THE GANG OF FOUR

Four Leaders. Four Communities. One Friendship.

By Bob Santos and Gary Iwamoto

Bob Santos, Bernie Whitebear, Larry Gossett, and Roberto Maestas. Photo courtesy UIATF

Publication of The *Gang of Four* is made possible through the generous support of
The Muckleshoot Indian Tribe, located in Auburn, Washington.

©2015 by Chin Music Press

Chin Music Press
1501 Pike Place #329
Seattle, WA 98101
www.chinmusicpress.com

Library of Congress Cataloging in Publication Data is available.

Written by Bob Santos and Gary Iwamoto
Edited by Elaine Ikoma Ko
Designed by Zeus Design
Website by Sean Muliro
Printed and bound in Canada

CONTENTS

PREFACE

by Bob Santos
Co-Author & Gang of Four Member

This is a story of how an American Indian, African American, Mexican American, and Asian American came together to form a powerful political alliance. We became known as Seattle's Gang of Four--Roberto Maestas, Bernie Whitebear, Larry Gossett and myself.

In the late sixties, I witnessed progressive movements beginning to emerge - around employment discrimination, equal education, exclusionary private "whites-only" clubs, and neighborhood preservation. The continuing unpopular war in Vietnam gave rise to a locally active anti-war movement.

The struggles faced by Native American fishermen, prevented from fishing on their traditional tribal fishing grounds in the rivers and open waters, led to the Indian Fishing Rights Movement. The fight for the Native Americans' right to fish in Washington waters began with the leadership of Bob Satiacum, a Puyallup Native American and fisherman by trade. Satiacum met Bernie Whitebear, a young inland Native American, and inspired Bernie to join the Indian Fishing Rights Movement.

Satiacum, Whitebear, other Native American leaders such as Billy Frank, Jr. and Al Bridges gained support from prominent national figures such as Marlon Brando, Jane Fonda, Buffy St. Marie and Dick Gregory. They helped bring the struggle for Indian fishing rights to national prominence on the evening news. Bernie's involvement in the fishing rights struggle was just the start of a lifetime of activism, serving the needs of urban Native Americans.

Larry Gossett, while a young VISTA volunteer, was assigned to serve in Harlem, New York. He learned the art of organizing and followed the writings and teachings of Malcolm X and Stokely Carmichael, which called for pride in the black power movement. Working in Harlem served as an awakening of Larry's political consciousness.

Upon his return to Seattle, Larry met with Elmer and Aaron Dixon (two brothers who started the local chapter of the Black Panther Party), E.J. Brisker, Carl Miller, Eddie Walker, Richard Brown, and Cathy Halley and together they formed the Black Student Union (BSU) at the University of Wasington (UW). In 1967, the BSU, under Larry's leadership, occupied the offices of University President Charles Odegaard, to force the administration to include African American studies and to hire more Black faculty members on staff. It wouldn't be the last time that Larry was involved in occupying buildings and offices in service to the community.

Roberto Maestas, a young teacher fresh out of UW, was an interested bystander when Larry Gossett and the BSU occupied Franklin High School. The BSU occupation at Franklin had a profound effect on Roberto. The demands made for a curriculum that included historical contributions by people of color and for hiring more minority teachers resonated with Roberto. It was soon after the occupation at Franklin that Roberto went back to school to join other Chicano activists involved in social and political movements.

When each of us were hired as Executive Directors of our respective community-based, non-profit agencies, we assumed a leadership role not only in the four organizations -- El Centro de la Raza, the United Indians of All Tribes Foundation (UIATF), the Central Area Motivation Program (CAMP) and the International District Improvement Association (Inter*Im) -- but in our respective communities as well.

We each spent decades working in our own communities, organizing the elderly, students, working people, property owners, business owners and activists to preserve culture and, in some cases, preserve entire neighborhoods, while fighting for equal rights in educational opportunities, employment, housing, women's rights, voting rights and immigrant rights.

Our paths often crossed at different times during the turbulent civil rights era that spanned the late sixties, seventies, and eighties up to the present time.

We joined each other's political and social justice causes. We met often to share our accomplishments and to socialize, which in later years, was often. Much of our conversations were socially directed, or 'mis-directed' might I say, with much teasing between Bernie and Roberto or Roberto and me. And we all liked to 'mess' with a gullible Larry.

The bond that we shared was unique. We realized, as time went on, that our shared vision and collective influence needed to be preserved.   Soon after Bernie passed away in 2000, Roberto, Larry, and I decided that because our relationship was so unique and potentially inspiring to others, we should document our collective experiences.

Each of us contributed to the development of this book. Roberto was interviewed and shared his insights before he passed away. with the assistance of Estela Ortega, Roberto Maestas' wife, and Lawney Reyes provided childhood stories of his brother, Bernie Whitebear, through his two books about Bernie, "Bernie Whitebear: An Urban Indian's Quest for Justice" and "White Grizzly Bear's Legacy: Learning to be Indian."

Indeed, working on this book was a labor of love.

ABOUT CO-AUTHOR GARY IWAMOTO

Gary Iwamoto is a life-long resident of Seattle graduating from Franklin High School, and earning degrees in communications and law from the University of Washington.

Gary became active in the local Asian community soon after he graduated.

He was a member of the coram nobis legal team, which worked to successfully overturn the World War II convictions of Gordon Hirabayashi, who defied a military curfew and internment order.

He was a member of the legal team which held the Philippine's Ferdinand Marcos regime responsible for the murders of Seattle political activists Gene Viernes and Silme Domingo in 1981.

Gary is a contributing writer for the International Examiner, a local community newspaper. He has written plays produced by the Northwest Asian American Theatre and has written skits for the Gang of Four, which they performed at the Northwest Asian American Theatre's Community Show Off.

Gary co-authored with Bob Santos, *Hum Bows, Not Hot Dogs*, a memoir of Bob Santos' life, in 2002.

While this book is written in a "third person" voice, it was taken from the individuals' direct experiences. To write this story, Gary relied on several sources of information over an extended period of time. Larry Gossett, Bob Santos, and Roberto Maestas were interviewed together for several sessions and each were interviewed separately as well as provided written responses to interview questions.

Lawney Reyes provided childhood stories of his brother, Bernie Whitebear, through his two books about Bernie, "*Bernie Whitebear: An Urban Indian's Quest for Justice*" and "*White Grizzly Bear's Legacy: Learning to be Indian.*"

Gary also obtained many newspaper accounts of the historical events that are featured in the book.

FOREWORD

I was very fortunate to be living in Oakland, California and to attend San Francisco State College in the latter 1960s. It was then that the civil rights and anti-war movements were peaking in the Bay Area. Community activism, particularly among students, was surging even amid the hippie counter-culture scene.

At San Francisco State, I attended every noon rally during the student strike in 1968 and joined other students in boycotting classes. The strike lasted five months and was led by the Third World Liberation Front. While the coalition was led by the Black Students Union (the first such in the country), it included Chicano American, Chinese American, and Native American student groups.

I was very glad with the unity of racial groups and equally impressed with their principle of "self-determination," which dictated that racial minorities make their own decisions, and determine their own destiny without others (i.e. whites). Of course, I completely agreed with their demands, which included the establishment of ethnic studies programs, increased enrollment of minority students, hiring of more minority faculty, financial aid and program support for minority students. I was elated when the administration finally gave in to these just demands. It showed me what could be accomplished when racial groups unite for causes that provide mutual benefits to each group.

However, when I returned to Seattle in the early 1970s, it appeared to me that there was not much networking nor organized efforts to get racial groups working together.

Back in the late 1940s, there was the multi-racial Jackson Street Community Council, which was established to bridge differences between racial groups and to improve the economic and physical conditions in what is now called the Chinatown/International District and much of the Central Area. That area was largely a racial enclave where many of the African Americans and Asian Americans resided at the time. The Council, which was funded by United Good Neighborhood (which later became United Way), has been credited with some success as a community action organization since it was able to get the "ear" of the City officials, managed to pass some ordinances dealing with blight in the neighborhood, and brought about racial harmony in the city.
In the sixties, however, the Jackson Street Community Council gave way to the more powerful and compelling civil rights movement that gripped the nation. It also gave way to racial and ethnic nationalism, and conflict. Many Asian Americans and others fled the Central Area as many younger Blacks protested and rebelled against others in their struggle for equality and "Black Power."

But as the civil rights movement progressed, there was a growing segment of the population that acknowledged America's history of discrimination and prejudice towards African Americans and sympathetic to their struggle for equal rights, treatment, and opportunity. They included a growing segment of Asian Americans, Latino American, and Native Americans, who recognized that they too were minorities, that they were also secondary citizens and objects of racial discrimination and prejudice. They too wanted to become involved in the civil rights movement and to expand it to their own to bring attention to their own problems and issues.

Subsequently, each community of color more or less established their own movement and went their own separate way to improve their lot and to meet their needs.

Clearly, racial unity is Seattle had a long way to go when I returned to Seattle in 1972. I lived with my parents at the Beacon Hill Junction upon my return.

Coincidentally, the Asian Drop-In Center was located at the house next door and the old Beacon Hill Elementary School was just across the street. So I got to know a number of the Asian American student activists, who were engaged in the Chinatown-International District and the King County domed stadium issue and got involved with the Third World Coalition, who met at El Centro de la Raza (old Beacon Hill Elementary School).

I connected with the members of the Gang of Four shortly after my return to Seattle. I got to know Bob Santos, who had just became director of the International District Improvement Association (Inter*Im) at the time, and after attending some board meetings, I became a member of the board of that agency.

I met Roberto Maestas and Larry Gossett through the Third World Coalition. The Coalition became involved in a number of issues around Puget Sound, including Indian Fishing Rights, the domed stadium and the preservation of the International District, the grape boycott and the struggle of the United Farm Workers, Chicano Studies, jobs for minority youth, construction jobs for minorities, the acquisition of El Centro, city funding for minority programs, and a lot of other causes affecting communities of color.

Bob, Roberto and Larry and others all joined Tyree Scott and the United Construction Workers in closing down a number of public construction sites in the area because of the lack of minority workers on those jobs. I did not meet Bernie Whitebear until some time later, but knew of his fight to secure land for urban Native Americans at what was Fort Lawton and now called Discovery Park, and to secure the old Sick's Seattle Stadium.

Roberto, Bob, Larry and Bernie...each of them developed effective agencies that not only provides a comprehensive range of needed services and programs, but also organizations that became powerful voices for their respective communities. At the same time, each of them maintained their relentless fight for social and economic justice. When they began supporting each other and collaborating, they became the "Gang of Four' or the "Four Amigos," a dynamic Third World force. Together, the unity of communities of color coming together to determine their own destiny.

Each of them have left an indelible mark on Seattle and beyond as this book so compellingly describes. Each will go down in history among Seattle's prominent civil rights leaders, joining the likes of Chief Sealth, Horace Cayton, Gordon Hirabayashi, Wing Luke, and Tyree Scott. Already there have been streets, buildings, and housing projects named after each of them.

We have indeed been blessed to have these legends who fought for racial and economic justice for all.

Doug Chin
Activist, Historian, Writer
Seattle, Washington

EARLY LIFE:
LOVE AND SURVIVAL
Part I

BOB SANTOS

CHAPTER 1 – Life in the Early Chinatown Days

The press called him "Sockin' Sammy Santos." Sammy's success in the ring was a source of pride for the local Filipino American community. During the late 1920's, boxer Sammy Santos fought as a lightweight in California, Oregon, and Ohio, then ended up in Seattle, a popular fight town in the old days. He had earned a reputation of toughness, armed with a tremendous punching ability.

Unfortunately, Sammy never made it to the top. He came close, one fight away from a championship bout, but never won the "big one."

Like Sammy, young single Filipino males had come to America in the 1920's and 1930's with dreams of making their fortunes. They became part of an itinerant migrant labor force that worked the Alaska canneries and West Coast farmlands.

Seattle's Chinatown was a natural stopping off place for those resting between the cannery and the fields. Given the residential segregation laws prevalent in the city, the area was one of the few in the city where Filipinos could live.

One of Sammy's hangouts in Chinatown was the Rizal Cafe where a young beautiful Filipina waitress named Virginia Nicol caught his eye and his heart.

Sammy and Virginia were married in 1931. In 1932, soon after Sammy retired from the ring, they had a son, Sammy Junior, (he was called Sammy Boy). In 1934, a second son, Robert Nicholas, was born. But everyone would call him Bobby.

Tragically, soon after Bobby was born, his mother Virginia was diagnosed with tuberculosis. She deteriorated rather quickly and died at the young age of 23 in 1935. Little Bobby never got to know his mother. His only memories of her were from pictures Sammy had kept.

Sammy Santos, the young widower, found it very difficult to raise two young energetic boys, so he reached out to the in-laws for help. The oldest, Sammy Boy, went to live with relatives in Tacoma. The youngest, Bobby, went to live with his Aunt Toni (Virginia's sister) and Uncle Joe Adriatico in an apartment on Spruce Street, in the Central Area. They had two children of their own, Adela and Joe Paul, as well as Patrick, an adopted cousin. Little Bobby was warmly welcomed as one of the family.

Uncle Joe came from a well-connected political family in the Philippines. Joe's father, Macario, was a political foe of Manuel Quezon, the first president of the Republic of the Philippines. Joe was a well-read, politically savvy man with common sense views. It was he, more than anyone else, who first shaped Bobby's early political awareness.

Aunt Toni was a very generous woman and a devout Catholic. She volunteered her time to help the poor and she took in and provided for foster children. At the age of six, Bobby started parochial school, attending the Maryknoll School for kindergarten.

Seattle's Chinatown was an exciting world for young Bobby Santos. It was a cosmopolitan area where not only the Filipinos called home but was also home to the Chinese and Japanese immigrants.

Bobby and brother Sam in 1935. Photo courtesy Santos collection

When Bobby was old enough, he stayed with his father on the weekends and holidays in Chinatown. Bobby looked up to his father. He memorized each page of his father's worn out boxing scrapbook and knew every boxer Sammy had knocked out and what round.

But the fighting took its toll on Sammy. His eyesight grew increasing worse, ultimately becoming blind. Bobby had to become his father's eyes. Sammy lived in Room 306, a small apartment that measured nine by 13 feet in the N.P. Hotel, named after the Northern Pacific Railway, in the heart of what was then known as Japantown.

Each Saturday, Bobby took his father by the arm to visit his father's favorite hangouts in Chinatown: the Jackson Cafe or the Paramount Cafe for breakfast, the barber shops for a shave and haircut, Duke's II for beer, the Filipino Improvement Club for lunch, a bathhouse for an afternoon soak, and the Bataan Recreation Club for visits with friends.

One of Bobby's earliest memories was seeing Judy Garland in the Wizard of Oz in 1940 at the Atlas Theater on Maynard Avenue South. For ten cents, Bobby was hooked on Saturday matinee movie serials featuring the adventures of Flash Gordon and Buck Rogers. He was frightened and entranced by kabuki dancers at the Nippon Kan Theater. Higo's was a popular novelty store where a dime bought a couple of comic books with a couple of pennies to spare for candy. Ice cream treats could be had at Chick's Ice Creamery in a storefront at the Bush Hotel.

Chinese food, Japanese food, Filipino food, and American food--it didn't matter--Bobby had his choice of restaurants and cuisine. There was the Paramount Cafe, the Golden Pheasant, across the street from the N.P. Hotel on Sixth Avenue South, Gyokko-Ken at Fifth Avenue South and South Main, Don Ting Restaurant, and the Hong Kong Restaurant on Maynard, very popular with the Filipino 'Alaskeros' (Alaskan cannery workers) because it was located in the center of what was considered Manilatown.

Early life in Seattle was good for young Bobby.

> *"It was he (Uncle Joe), more than anyone else, who first shaped Bobby's early political awareness."*

Infant Bobby and his mother Virginia Nichol.
Photo courtesy Santos collection

CHAPTER 2: "I Am Filipino" and Filipino Bunkhouses

Japan's attack on Pearl Harbor on December 7, 1941, had a direct effect on Bobby Santos. Young Bobby was in the middle of the first grade at the Maryknoll School, a Catholic missionary church and school. Japanese American kids made up the majority of students at the school, with the rest from Filipino families who lived in the neighborhood.

After the attack on Pearl Harbor, anti-Japanese hysteria forced the evacuation of all Japanese, citizen and alien alike, from the West Coast. The Japanese community was devastated -- their possessions, homes and businesses were sold for a fraction of their worth. They could only keep the possessions they were able to carry into the internment camps.

Bobby witnessed his Japanese American friends and their families leave the neighborhood, put on buses which would take them to "relocation centers" for the duration of the war. The Maryknoll School was closed. Bob understood that America was at war with Japan. But America was also at war with Germany and Italy. And yet, Bobby wondered then, why weren't the German and Italian families forced to evacuate as well?

After the Maryknoll School closed, Bobby entered the second grade at the Immaculate Conception School in the fall of 1942. Even though all of the Japanese American families had been evacuated and removed from the neighborhood, strong feelings of anti-Japanese sentiment remained.

At the age of eight, young Bobby had his first real personal experience with racism and prejudice.

During one lunch period, a boy grabbed Bobby and yelled, "Are you a Jap, huh, are you a Jap?" Crying, Bobby answered, "No, honest, I'm a Filipino." These kinds of incidents were common and not too long after, Asian American kids in Bobby's neighborhood wore badges printed "I AM FILIPINO" or "I AM CHINESE."

Most Saturday nights, Bobby and his friends could be found at Filipino community dances held at the Washington Hall at 14th Avenue South and Fir Street or at Finnish Hall on Washington Street. The dances brought out all the single Filipino guys who always outnumbered the Filipino women and girls. Bobby and his friends always knew the latest and popular dance styles--the jitterbug, swing, and the offbeat.

As a teen, Bobby worked at waiting tables at the Navy Officers' Club, washing dishes at the G.O. Guy Drugs, or cleaning clam nectar pots at the original Ivar's Acres of Clams restaurant on the waterfront.

A "slimer" was a job that nobody wanted.

Getting a ticket to the canneries in Alaska was a valuable commodity, an opportunity to make a lot of money in a short period of time. Cannery workers were guaranteed $1,200 plus overtime for the season. As a seventeen year old, Bobby had no seniority. But he was the son of Sammy Santos, which carried some weight and favor with Gene Navarro, the union dispatcher. Bobby went to the canneries as Gene's protégé.

Bobby spent two summers in the canneries. He was assigned to place tops on the cans of fish, then load the cans into boxes for shipment, eight hours a day, during the six-week season from the beginning of June to mid-August. It was hard work.

In the second summer, he was assigned the job of "slimer." A "slimer" was a job that nobody wanted. As the fish went down the conveyor belts, butchers lopped off the heads and split the fish lengthwise. Slimers stood at workstations with faucets, cleaned out the guts, and placed the cut fish into cans. Slimers worked until the fishing boats were empty.

Bobby got another first-hand experience with racism. The white workers--fishermen and mechanics--lived in a series of single house duplexes while the Filipino workers were crammed into bunkhouses, eight to a room. The whites enjoyed a menu of steak, pork chops, BLTs, waffles, eggs, bacon, and turkey while the Filipinos were fed fish and rice daily, with chicken only on Sundays.

Bobby was not to realize until later how these experiences shaped his political consciousness.

CHAPTER 3: Early Pursuit of the American Dream

In 1952, after graduating from high school, Bob (no longer "Bobby") joined the Marine Corps for a three-year hitch while the Korean War was still in progress. He went through basic training, learning to be an aircraft mechanic. But shortly before he completed basic training, the armistice was signed and the Korean War was over. Still eager to fight, Bob joined the boxing team. He won a few fights but his experiences didn't encourage him to go professional.

In October of 1955, Bob was discharged from the Marine Corps and came home to Seattle. It didn't take him long to find a job and he was hired by the Boeing Company. Bob was assigned to the hammer shop at Boeing's Renton plant as a hammer operator's assistant. Fortunately for Bob, his shop foreman was an old boxing fan who remembered Sammy Santos from his boxing days, more than 25 years earlier. The foreman took Bob under his wing and gave him an opportunity for advancement, once again, benefiting from being Sammy's son.

Postcard from Seattle World's Fair 1962. Image courtesy Century 21

In 1957, he had been promoted at the hammer shop to hammer operator. He had met and fallen in love with Anita Agbalog, a recent graduate of Franklin High School who had been working the summers at one of Bob's favorite hangouts, the Manila Cafe in Chinatown. She too had found a job at Boeing's as a graphic designer. It was a whirlwind romance. After less than a year of courtship, Bob proposed marriage to Anita. She agreed and the young couple started married life together in a small apartment at 14th Avenue and Spring Street in the Central Area.

But Bob, still working at the Boeing Company, started having problems at work. He had been involved in an ongoing conflict with a white union steward, a forklift operator, who was jealous of Bob's close relationship with the shop foreman. The forklift operator deliberately rammed into Bob. In response, Bob went after the union steward, knocking him into a pile of discarded metal. Bob was arrested and charged with assault and battery. When Bob went to trial, others in the shop provided testimony that it was the forklift operator who had provoked the incident. Bob was acquitted but he knew his days at the Boeing Company were numbered.

So Bob decided to invest in a barbecue restaurant with childhood friends Ben and Eddie Laigo, called "The Rib Pit." They had ambitious plans. With thousands of tourists coming to the 1962 Seattle World's Fair, Bob and the Laigo brothers believed that they could make a lot of money. They decided to sponsor a three-night jazz concert featuring the Dave Brubeck group at the Green Lake Aqua Theater. They brought in local talent such as the Joni Metcalf Trio and Teddy Ross, who years later, won a Tony Award for his role as the Cowardly Lion in "The Wiz" on Broadway. But nobody came. Bob and the Laigo brothers took a big hit financially, closed their restaurant, and declared bankruptcy.

As the decade of the sixties went on and took on a turbulent tone, Bob's career path was about to take a dramatic turn. He was about to discover his true identity and calling: Uncle Bob—Community Activist.

He was about to discover his true identity and calling: Uncle Bob-- Community Activist.

The Santos family in 1966, Front: Simone, John, and Robin Middle: Anita and Bob Back: Tommy and Danny. Photo courtesy of the Santos family.

Working together, the "Four Amigos" have been among the most influential and charismatic leaders in our community. Since the late 1960s, their activism for social justice and civil rights has changed the face of leadership in the Puget Sound region, inspiring generations. Theirs is a unique story of diverse communities working together to fully integrate minorities into the area's social, economic and political life.

A.K. Guy
Award Committee

Bernie's father, Julian Reyes, was born in the Philippines in 1895, and left the Philippines by boat at the age of 17, arriving in the United States in 1912. Like many young Filipinos such as Sammy Santos, he had come to America to seek his fortune. He found work in the Alaska canneries.

BERNIE WHITEBEAR

CHAPTER 4: A Proud Family

He lived for a time in Seattle during the 1920s but left, traveling to Idaho and Montana to find work and eventually ended up in Inchelium, in Eastern Washington.

The town of Inchelium was a gathering place for the Colville and Lakes Indian tribes. The tribes had settled there after being forced to move after the white people had taken their lands in the Colville valley and in the northern half of what is now the Colville Reservation.

Bernie Daybreak Star circa 1980s. Photo courtesy UIATF

Bernie's mother, Mary Christian, was the niece of James Bernard, chief of the Lakes tribe. He had been his tribe's leader for more than thirty years. Later, he would travel to Washington DC on three occasions to negotiate a reservation land base and to advocate for the rights of his tribe. He eventually died of a heart attack.

Mary's mother, Teresa Christian, James Bernard's sister, had died of pneumonia, when Mary was five and her father, Alex Christian, died of tuberculosis, when she was eleven.

Alex was a very revered member of the tribe. He had earned a reputation as a skilled hunter. It was said that once, while on a hunting trip, Alex had encountered a white grizzly bear and was struck by its magnificence and beauty. He refused to kill the creature and vowed never to hunt such a creature out of respect.

When the tribe learned of his noble gesture, they gave him the name of *Pic Ah Kelowna* or White Grizzly Bear, a name we would hear more about.

Orphaned by the loss of her parents, Mary went to live with Charles and Eliza Hall until she was sixteen when she met and married Julian Reyes in 1930. Julian was 35 years old, nineteen years older than Mary. Julian was accepted as a member of the tribe and quickly adjusted to the way of life on the reservation. A son, Lawney, was born in 1931, and daughter Luana was born in 1933.

In 1935, construction began on the Grand Coulee Dam. The structure blocked the traditional migration of salmon in the Columbia River, destroying the livelihood of the Lakes (Sin-Aikst), the Colville (Swhy-ayl-push) and other Indian tribes, which had depended on salmon as their major food source. The roots, berries, nuts and herbs, which nourished the tribes, were flooded with the raising of the Columbia River.

The construction of the Grand Coulee Dam brought change. A town immediately sprang up by the dam. Thousands of construction workers came to town to work on the project. Small frame buildings were built to house the many businesses which opened to cater to the needs of these workers --taverns, grocery stores, hotels, dance halls, and restaurants.

Julian and Mary decided to open a Chinese restaurant by the Grand Coulee Dam. But they knew very little about Chinese cuisine. As fate would have it, a Chinese man named Harry Wong, walked into the restaurant one day and ordered some food. Curious about the man, Julian and Mary Introduced themselves to Harry and found out that Harry had just come from Spokane, knew how to cook, and was looking for a job. Harry was hired on the spot!

Soon, the three worked closely together--Harry cooking, Julian washing the dishes and buying the supplies, and Mary waitressing and serving as cashier.

In early 1937, Julian and Mary decided to leave the Grand Coulee Dam area to return to the Colville Reservation. Mary was pregnant. They sold the restaurant to Harry Wong and came back to Inchelium. Needing work, they eventually were hired by the Colville tribe to be fireguards in the Gold Mountain area for the summer. The family lived in a tent near the summit to the mountain.

On September 25, 1937, Julian took Mary to the Colville Indian Agency Hospital in Nespelem, Washington. Two days later, she gave birth to a baby boy. She decided to name the baby, "Bernard," in honor of her uncle, Chief of the Lakes Tribe James Bernard. Bernard Reyes would eventually become Bernie Whitebear.

Young Bernie grew up in poverty. He spent his childhood in Eastern Washington on the Colville reservation. His family was constantly on the move, looking for work on the apple orchards or on the railroad. Bernie spent much of his early youth, living out of a tent, accompanying his parents on their nomadic quest to make ends meet. He grew up in the shadow of the Grand Coulee Dam, a monumental accomplishment for the development of energy but which also destroyed the way of life, which Indians had enjoyed for over a hundred years.

As the summer drew to a close, their jobs as fireguards ended, Julian and Mary packed up their tent and their three young children and drove the family's Model T toward the apple orchards outside of Omak, "white man's territory." Julian and Mary found jobs as apple pickers but were constantly harassed by young white men who drove by and shouted racial obscenities at them because of the color of their skin. Luana, Lawney, and Pickles, the family's dog, took care of little Bernie. Julian kept a gun handy when the family slept.

After the apple-picking season was over, the Reyes family once again packed up and drove off in their Model T, back toward Inchelium. On the way back, the family stopped off at a rest stop. Pickles, the family dog, jumped out of the car. A car, with four young white men, purposely ran over Pickles. The family was shocked! They dug a shallow grave, laid their beloved family pet to rest, and drove solemnly on.

Julian Reyes spent long hours, working on a small wood-framed house, building a shed, digging a cellar, which became a storehouse for vegetables and a playground for the three children. But while Julian solidified the foundation for the family home, his marriage to Mary began to crumble and she suddenly left the family in the spring of 1939. Maybe it was the age difference-- Julian was forty-five years old, Mary was twenty-six years old.

Little Bernie was left in the care of his older sister Luana. Luana was only six years old and she tried her best. She washed her little brother, combed his hair, fed him breakfast, brushed his teeth, and bathed him. She helped prepare the family meals.
In 1940, after ten years of marriage, Mary filed for divorce from Julian. Bernie, at the age of two years old, was too young to understand what was happening.

Judge Brown granted Mary a divorce but made a ruling on custody that made nobody happy. He determined that neither parent could properly afford to care for the three children. Although the judge gave custody of the children to Julian, Luana and Lawney were ordered to attend an off-reservation boarding school.

Young Bernie was sent to live with Mary's foster parents, Charlie and Eliza Hall. Julian would have custody over Bernie on the weekends when he wasn't working. Mary did get visitation rights. She wasn't happy by the decision but didn't have the money to appeal the custody order.

As the fall of 1940 approached, Lawney and Luana learned that Judge Brown had sent them to attend the Chemawa Indian School near Salem, Oregon. Now, young Bernie had to not only adjust to life without his mother but also had to adjust to life without his siblings.

Life wasn't so good for young Bernie. During the weekdays, he lived with the Halls. His father was constantly gone, in search of odd jobs here and there. No children lived near them so Bernie had no playmates. He greatly missed his mother, sister, and brother. He did have Brownie, the family dog, for company. Because his son was so lonely, Julian bought a goat to keep Bernie company. Bernie named the goat, "Goat!"

The Halls were elderly and in frail health. Like many families in Inchelium, the Halls were poor. Bernie wore pants with patches covering holes, ragged shirts, and well-worn shoes.

The salmon, which had been a major staple, had stopped running when the Columbia River was dammed. Bernie never had fresh milk and often went without eating. Fresh vegetables were only available during the summer. Friends often helped out, giving Julian beans, cornmeal, and macaroni to help feed his son.

In early 1941, Julian secured a loan from the tribe and with the help of friends, built a new house. He built a two-room house near a running creek, but it had no running water or electricity.

When the summer came, Lawney and Luana finally came home. Bernie spent the entire summer, tagging along after Lawney or having Luana read to him. His playgrounds were the forests, creeks, and rivers where his father worked. He learned about fishing and hunting from his brother and about nature from his sister.

Such was young Bernie's early life.

CHAPTER 5: Tents, Chandeliers and "Siwash"

Bernie was becoming curious about the world around him. On December 7, 1941, Japan bombed Pearl Harbor. With no playmates of his own age, Bernie spent much time in the company of his father and his father's friends. As the adults talked about the impending war with Japan, Bernie listened intently. He had never seen a Japanese person. He curiously asked his father who the Japanese were and why they bombed Pearl Harbor.

In 1943, Julian decided to give young Bernie a taste of the big city. The Reyes family took a trip to Spokane. It was a wondrous new world for Bernie. He saw his first street light. He saw the biggest building he had ever seen in his young life, the Montana Hotel, in the poor section of Spokane.

He was introduced to his first indoor toilet and was so fascinated that he flushed it again and again. He saw his first movie, a cartoon with Bugs Bunny and Elmer Fudd, and enjoyed his first taste of popcorn. He saw another movie, a Western, where Bernie and Lawney were the only ones in the theater rooting for the Indians.

Bernie, upper Hall Creek, Inchelium WA
Photo courtesy UIATF

Later that day, on a visit to the Natorium Park, the biggest amusement park in the Inland Empire, a white man threw Lawney out because he looked like a "Jap."

Julian told the man, "He's not a Jap, he's an Indian." The man said, "Well, I guess that's better than being a Jap."

On the trip home to Inchelium, Bernie and Lawney talked among themselves. Why, Bernie asked Lawney, did the man think you were Japanese? Lawney, as bewildered as Bernie, didn't know. All they knew was that America was at war with the Japan and that the Japanese lived very far away, across the Pacific Ocean.

In the fall of 1943, Bernie started school in Inchelium. With his natural curiosity, he was an avid learner. His sister Luana had prepared him for school, reading daily to him.

Bernie found that he liked school and he easily made friends. And finally, he had friends of his own age.

In 1944, the Reyes family was again on the move. Julian had found work as a Spanish interpreter for an apple grower in the Okanogan Valley who had hired two hundred non-English speaking Mexican pickers. The family lived in two cabins, one cabin for sleeping and one cabin for cooking, eating, and studying, with electricity but no running water. There was a large communal building for showering and laundering with toilets and sinks.

The Mexican laborers lived in two large warehouses converted to housing. One night, with about a week left in the apple harvest season, a fire broke out and consumed one of the warehouses. The Mexican laborers, who had been sleeping, barely got out, many with only the shirts on their backs. They lost everything, including all of the wages they had earned at the orchard.

When Julian, Lawney, and Bernie came upon the scene in the morning, most of the laborers were huddled under blankets, clad only in undershirts, in tears.

The sight of these hardworking men in despair had a profound effect on Bernie. He wanted to do something to ease their pain. He searched the charred remains to look for salvageable items but could not find any. It was a memory and a feeling he wouldn't forget--when you see others in pain, do something to ease that pain.

The Reyes family worked hard and saved enough money to buy a house and in 1948, they put a down payment on a house, which cost $750. The house had electricity but no running water. A water pump was located right next to the house. An outhouse stood behind the house. It was small but it was a home they could call their own.

In 1951, Bernie and Lawney decided to go to Tacoma to visit their mother and sister. Their mother had married Harry Wong, their longtime family friend, and had three children of their own. They hitchhiked, taking rides from five different strangers and made it in 11 hours. Bernie met his three step-siblings for the first time--five-year-old Junior (Harry), four-year-old Teresa, and three- year-old Laura. Bernie and Lawney stayed the summer, getting to know their new extended family.

In 1953, sixteen-year-old Bernie had saved enough money to buy his first car, a 1934 Ford Coupe. He had grown to be a gregarious, popular young man. Even though he often was the only Indian in his classes, Bernie was very popular. His easy-going manner, warm personality, and self-deprecating humor attracted people to him. Having a car helped as well, especially in the fifties.

Like many teenagers of the day, Bernie was interested in learning how to dance-- at the Sawdust Maker's Hall in Omak, the Riverside Hall, Brewster Open Pavilion, Maple Hall, or hanging out at the Daisy Mae Drive In, serving the greatest hamburgers in the Okanogan Valley. And especially, checking out members of the opposite sex.

Almost all of Bernie's high school friends were white. He made friendships that lasted his entire life. He was treated as one of the crowd. But it was their parents who looked down on Bernie. They did not want their sons and daughters associated with a "Siwash," a derogatory term that whites used against Indians in stereotyping them as dirty, lazy, and shiftless.

Bernie knew that he and his white friends lived in different worlds. When he was invited by his friends to their homes, he found they lived with running water and indoor plumbing, oak floors, chandeliers, well manicured lawns, and lush drapes which covered large picture windows. It was so different to what he had grown up with.

Bernie's first girlfriend was an attractive girl - a blonde blue-eyed girl named Marilyn Hodgson. He spent a lot of time with her during his high school days. They were an item yet he was not welcome in her home. In fact, her parents tried their best to break up their relationship, and later it eventually ended. Later, Bernie met the love of his life--Marilyn Sieber. Bernie met Marilyn, a member of the Nit Nat tribe located near Victoria, British Columbia, during the early days of the United Indians of All Tribe Foundation. They were together for ten years. At one time, Bernie announced plans to marry Marilyn but they never did. She eventually moved back to Canada.

In 1955, Bernie graduated from Okanogan High School. Good paying jobs in the Okanogan Valley were scarce for young Indians. He decided to go to the coast to see if he could find a job. He moved in with his mother Mary and her second family in Tacoma. After weeks of searching for a job, he gave up and went back to the Okanogan Valley. With his father Julian's help, Bernie found a summer job with the Great Northern Railroad. He saved enough money for tuition to enter the UW in the fall.

Bernie & Marilyn

Bernie and Marilyn Sieber circa 1970s. Photo courtesy UIATF

In the summer of 1956, after just one year of college, Bernie decided not to return to the UW. He hadn't done well in his studies and had not found a field of study that interested him.

CHAPTER 6: Bernie Meets His Mentor

One day that summer in 1956, Bernie met a man named Bob Satiacum, a friend of Bernie's mother, who was a regular customer at Harry Wong's Tacoma restaurant. Satiacum was a local Indian legend. He was a striking figure, six feet tall with an athletic build. He was unlike any person Bernie had ever known. Bernie was a country boy at heart while Bob Satiacum was a savvy, city slicker. Bob promised to introduce Bernie to some of his Indian friends.

Bernie continued to look for work that summer without success and he again ran into Satiacum. After Bernie confided how hard it was to find work, Satiacum offered to take him drift net fishing for salmon in the nearby Puyallup River. Bernie had never fished for salmon before. He knew how to fish with a pole but this was an entirely new experience for him. Bernie took Satiacum up on his offer.

It was the beginning of a life-long friendship.

Satiacum became a mentor for Bernie. Satiacum taught Bernie everything he knew about salmon--how to prepare it for cooking, how to cut it, and how to smoke it with a strong alder fire. Bernie developed a taste for Indian alder smoked salmon. Satiacum lent Bernie a canoe and they went salmon fishing in Commencement Bay. All the while, Satiacum told Bernie about Indian treaties that had been signed in the 1850s when Washington State was still a territory, which gave Indians the right to fish for salmon.

Bernie found that white sports fishermen resented their presence and often tried to sabotage their fishing nets. Bernie had experienced some hostility from whites while he was growing up in Eastern Washington but not to the level he experienced in Western Washington. Satiacum told Bernie that whites in Eastern Washington tolerated Native Americans because they were no threat to them but it was different in Western Washington. Confrontations were commonplace. Satiacum carried a shotgun in his canoe. Bernie started carrying an ax handle, just in case, for protection.

Bernie decided to change his last name to Grizzly White Bear, in honor of his grandfather, Alex Christian, who was known among the Lake tribes as Chief White Grizzly Bear.

Salmon was a valuable commodity and the white commercial fishermen depended on the salmon for profits. The white sports fishermen viewed the salmon as their property. The Native American fishermen needed the salmon to sustain their way of life. Native Americans had fished for salmon long before the white man entered the territory. But commercial fishing had taken its tolls. Salmon runs had become dangerously depleted. State authorities, particularly the State Fish and Wildlife Commission, took the position that drift net fishing violated the law. Satiacum had been arrested many times for "illegal" fishing without a state permit on the Puyallup River.

Bernie with actress and activist, Jane Fonda. Photo courtesy UIATF

In 1959, Bernie had finished a tour of duty with the U.S. Army. While he was encouraged to re-enlist for a second tour of duty, he decided to return to Tacoma and get involved in the Indian Fishing Rights Movement. After he returned to his mother's home in Tacoma, Bernie was hired to work at the Boeing Company, assigned to Plant Two, fabricating parts for jets.

In 1961, Bernie had resumed his friendship with Bob Satiacum. He spent a lot of his free time with Satiacum, who introduced Bernie to other urban Native Americans, particularly members of the Puyallup, Muckleshoot and Nisqually tribes. He encouraged Bernie to embrace his Native American heritage. Although Bernie carried the name of his Filipino father, Reyes, he had always identified himself as Indian. But for many years, Bernie had taken his Indian heritage for granted. Growing up in Eastern Washington, Bernie was familiar with living in poverty but didn't realize then the political and social implications involved.

Every so often, the Indians in Tacoma held a pow wow where they would celebrate their heritage through traditional dancing and drumming, handed down from generation to generation. These pow wows brought the various Indian groups together. It also served as a means for the younger generation of Indian youth to learn about and preserve their culture. The Indian elders were afraid their youth would lose the cultural connection to their past.

In the summer of 1961, Bernie joined his mother, his brother Lawney, and his sister Luana at a meeting of the Colville Indians held in Seattle. The meeting had been called to discuss the merits of terminating the Colville Indian reservation. There were about 150 people at the meeting, most of whom had relocated to Seattle. The U.S. government wanted to open up the reservation land in Eastern Washington to logging and mining companies because of the rich natural resources on reservation land. The government was offering $60,000 to each tribal member. It was a lot of money and although the offer was tempting, the Colville tribe voted unanimously to reject the offer.

Bernie was relieved.

Bernie decided to change his last name to Grizzly White Bear, in honor of his grandfather, Alex Christian, who was known among the Lake tribes as Chief White Grizzly Bear.

But White Grizzly Bear wouldn't fit on Bernie's Boeing employee nametag! Thus, Bernie shortened his last name. For the rest of his life, he would be known as Bernie Whitebear.

Bernie Whitebear

ROBERTO MAESTAS
CHAPTER 7: Humble New Mexican Roots

Roberto Maestas took pride in being an underdog. No one who looked at Roberto's

humble beginnings would have predicted any measure of success for a kid from a small

New Mexico village. For Roberto, adversity was a way of life. He never knew his parents. He

grew up on the poor side of town, having to share food and space with an extended family

of seventeen. And when he decided that he was old enough to leave, he left on a journey

to find himself. It was a journey, not only geographically but spiritually and politically, that

Roberto undertook that eventually led to Seattle, Washington.

Roberto, Seattle City Council Chamber early 1970s. Photo courtesy El Centro de la Raza

On July 9, 1938, Lina Maestas, had given birth to a son. She named him, Roberto. Located in the quaint little New Mexico village of San Agustine del Valle de Nuestra Senora de Lourdes, Isidoro and Emilia Vigil welcomed their youngest grandchild into the world and into their extended family.

Roberto's father, Francisco Maestas, had left the family, leaving Lina to raise a son, Francisco Jr., and a daughter, Mariana, by herself. Sadly, Lina Maestas was stricken with tuberculosis and lived only a few months after her youngest son Roberto was born.

The Vigils made a loving home for Roberto, Francisco Jr., and Mariana after their mother Lina fell ill and later became quarantined in a sanitarium in the southwestern part of the state. Roberto became the youngest of seventeen family members raised by Isidoro and Emilia Vigil -- the first generation of twelve sons and daughters, and the second generation, which included Roberto's brother and sister and two cousins.

With little knowledge of his mother or father, Roberto didn't understand why his parents weren't around. His mother had died and he didn't know why his father left. He often told people his father had died in the war. From his earliest memories, Roberto always lovingly referred to Isidoro as his daddy and Emilia as his momma.

Roberto looked up to his grandfather. Isidoro was a fearless man. He tamed wild horses, fought toe to toe with bulls trying to break down a fence, and wrestled goats to the ground to butcher their throats for food. He nonchalantly grabbed rattlesnakes by the tails and snapped them with a flick of the wrist. When Isidoro was eighty-six years old, he jumped on a wild horse. The horse threw Isidoro to the ground and kicked him in the head. He just got up, dusted himself off, and wiped the blood from the head. Emilia, however, held the undisputed power. It was she who kept the family together.

Isidoro and Emilia were very poor. The house was extremely cold in the wintertime with a small pot-bellied stove as the source of heat. There were three or four rooms in the house. The boys slept in one bedroom, the girls in one or two bedrooms, depending on how many of the seventeen being raised by Isidoro and Emilia were still in the house. As the years passed, some of Roberto's

Roberto, 1941 New Mexico. Photo courtesy El Centro de la Raza

extended family members began moving out to Texas or California. Despite having seventeen mouths to feed, Isidoro provided for his family. There were home grown vegetables. There were goats, chickens, and cattle. Each of the family members helped out. When Roberto was barely old enough to walk, he was given the important family responsibility of feeding the family's chickens and collecting eggs from the chicken coop.

The Vigil farmstead was one of several farmsteads in what was considered the village of San Agustine del Valle de Nuestra Senora de Lourdes, a village carved out of the Rocky Mountains in a box canyon, about a mile wide in a river valley about seven miles long. The nearest town, Las Vegas, with a population of 13,000 or so, was about fifteen miles away, above a mesa. The village was only accessible by a very steep rocky dirt road, which went down a 45-degree grade for about 1500 to 1800 feet from the mesa to the river valley below where San Agustine lay. The land was once part of the vast Mexican empire. Even after the territory became part of the United States, the Mexican heritage was acknowledged. It was called New Mexico for a reason.

There were perhaps twenty families who lived in or near the village. Every Sunday, the families walked or rode by horseback to the village where everybody gathered for church and a potluck or horse race after services. It was a close tight-knit community. All of the families, like the Lujans, the Gonzales', and the Vigils, were of Mexican descent. When the river flooded the homestead of one family, the other families pitched in to help out. When a cow wandered into the mountains and fell, looking for grazing, the villagers climbed the mountains to carve the cow and have a cook out for all the families.

In 1943, five-year-old Roberto learned that there was a world beyond his small village. He lived in a household where Spanish was the primary language spoken. In fact, almost everyone in the village spoke Spanish. He learned that one world was "nosotros" or "Los Mexicanos," and then there were the "gringos" who lived outside the village.

One day, one of Roberto's uncles who worked at a store in the nearby city of Las Vegas, New Mexico, brought home an outdated set of comic books, unsellable with their covers cut. These comic books, considered today to be classics, featured the popular cartoon characters of the 1940s--Superman, Batman, Wonder Woman, and Popeye, the Sailor Man. These comic books served as Roberto's introduction to the English language. Roberto was fascinated by the comics, immersing himself in these little treasures for hours on end. In the process, he began to learn the English language. The family had been using a Sears catalog for toilet paper and soon, Roberto spent time in the outhouse, trying to read the catalogue.

Once, Roberto went down by the river and took a comic book to read and fell asleep. When he woke up, he realized he was late for dinner. He knew he faced the wrath of his family. Everybody had to be at the table for breakfast, lunch, and dinner at the exact same time. Nobody would start eating until everybody was sitting down. All nineteen members of the family--Isidoro, Emilia, their six sons and six daughters, and five grandchildren had to wait for everyone to be seated.

Roberto was late and he knew it. So, when he finally showed up, he was asked where he was. He told his family, crying, replying in English, that he had been down by the river, looking for adventure. And everyone looked at him in surprise. Emilia, who didn't speak English at all, asked for a translation. Everybody laughed, thinking how cute and adorable Roberto, the youngest, was speaking that strange English!

Two of Roberto's uncles went to war. Both had fought in the Pacific and both were infected during their tour of duty with malaria and sent home. One of Roberto's uncles brought Roberto a map of the world and the other brought back a radio. Both the map and the radio broadened Roberto's sense of the world around him.

Roberto poured over that map, taking it out to look at the faraway places, putting it away, taking it out again and again. He'd look at the ocean and the countries with the amazing sounding names--Japan, Korea, Cuba, and Mexico and wondered if he could go to such places one day. And because the map was flat, Roberto thought the world was flat!
The radio was a thing of wonder, a crystallized battery-operated radio. The radio was used as an incentive to do the family chores. Roberto was told that if he did a good job in the garden or with the pigs or cows, he would be rewarded by given approval to play the radio in the heat of the day during the summer.

There was only one radio station near Roberto's homestead, broadcasting from the nearby town of Las Vegas. During the summer, the local radio station aired a daily broadcast of major league baseball games, but oddly, only the American League games. Baseball was the national pastime and a welcome diversion from news about the war. Roberto and Francisco and their friends became intrigued by this game of baseball.

Soon, they knew the names of each of the eight baseball teams in the American League.

Francisco told his brother and their friends to pick a team to root for, a team that would be his team for the rest of his life. Roberto picked the New York Yankees. Francisco told him that the Yankees were his team and that Roberto had to pick another team to root for. So they argued. They both wanted the Yankees. Finally, after Francisco smacked Roberto in the head, Roberto chose the Boston Red Sox. Of course, the Yankees won championship after championship while the Red Sox suffered in defeat. And each time the Yankees won, Francisco gloated at Roberto's expense.

Francisco (as Frank Maestas) later became an award-winning sports columnist and journalist for the Albuquerque Journal. He was called one of the most colorful sports writers in New Mexico sports history, whose passion for the Yankees and Notre Dame football was legendary.

In the fall of 1944, when Roberto was six years old, he was ready to start school. Roberto was excited about going to school. Most of his teachers were of Mexican descent, which was understandable since he lived on the Mexican side of town. He discovered that he enjoyed learning and couldn't wait for school to start.

While the little village had its own school, a single room for students from the first to the eighth grade with one teacher, Isidoro and Emilia didn't believe that the village school could provide a challenging education for the children. Isidoro sent Emilia and the children to the town of Las Vegas to go to school while he stayed behind on the farm, taking care of the pigs, the horses, and the livestock by himself. Roberto and his family members moved into a barrio, in a poverty stricken neighborhood where there never was enough space and where the water pipes froze in the wintertime.

Compared to the little village that Roberto lived in, the town of Las Vegas was in a different universe even though it was only fifteen miles away from the farm. After Roberto moved to Las Vegas, he had his first experience with the gringos and the differences between whites and Mexicans.

Las Vegas was separated, almost exactly in half by the Gallinas River. When Roberto was growing up, the town was totally segregated. On one side of the town, "La Plaza Nueva" or "New Town," the gringos lived in neighborhoods where all the nice homes were. All the department stores, such as the J.C. Penny's and Newberry's, as well as Highlands University, were in "New Town." On the other side of town, "La Plaza Vieja" or "Old Town," the Mexicans lived, mostly in tenement slums in the barrios. It was in Old Town where the taverns and the mental hospital were.

The Gallinas River served to separate the two worlds. The gringos never went to Old Town except to drink. The Mexicans never went to New Town unless they had business to do. The town was so segregated that each side had its own institutions--an all-white police department, school district, and political system in New Town and an all-Mexican police department, school district and political system in Old Town.

> Their super-hero natures were not recognized at that time by the majority of us. Instead they were disguised as troublesome challengers to what was for many, a comfortable system.

Virginia Anderson
Former Director, Seattle Center

CHAPTER 8: A Natural Leader

In 1947, young Roberto had his first paying job, delivering the Las Vegas Daily Optic. Roberto knew the route by heart because he had tagged along with his brother and uncle when they delivered the newspapers.

Roberto's paper route was considered the best paper route because the route took him to the fanciest homes and richest people, maybe 200 or so, in Las Vegas. They always paid on time. When Roberto went to collect for the newspaper, he looked in wonder when the doors opened at the white peoples' houses--fancy furniture, well-groomed carpets, and spacious rooms. He became fascinated with doorbells. The white people had manicured laws with green grass, even in the heat of the summertime. He was impressed that these houses had porches.

But the route also took him to the barrio, 20 or so customers, in the poorest part of town, back to his world of crowded spaces and makeshift furniture. They never paid on time and got behind on their payments. It was a struggle to collect the 25 cents a month subscription rate. It brought home to Roberto the disparity between the whites and the Mexicans. There was an old saying "the whites had all the gravy while the Mexicans had the beans."

Roberto had become very aware of his poverty. The soles of his shoes were so worn he often went to school with his shoes flapping. When the pipes froze, he couldn't wash his clothes and went to school without a clean pair of socks. He was so ashamed about his clothing that he pushed his pants down to hide that he wasn't wearing any socks.

But Roberto felt fortunate that he had a job, even though it didn't pay much, a few pennies a week from his paper route. His friends didn't have jobs. In fact, one of the most valuable commodities in Roberto's Mexican part of town was a job. Roberto had become a natural leader. He was assertive, daring, and adventuresome. Kids of his age gravitated to him. He had a group of five to ten close friends who did things together. There were two movie theaters in town, one in New Town, which showed mainstream Hollywood films, and one in Old Town, which showed films in Mexico. Both cost 16 cents admission. Add the price of a coke at a nickel, popcorn at a nickel a bag, and the total cost of a movie was 26 cents.

Each week provided a challenge for Roberto and his little gang to raise 26 cents for a movie. They found creative ways to raise the money--returning a soda bottle for deposit sometimes was worth ten cents. Begging money from Emilia worked sometimes but not all the time.

Then when Roberto turned 12, he and the other boys discovered girls. That meant having to raise 52 cents each week to bring the girl he wanted to impress to the movie theater. The boys had to become even more creative. For example, Roberto and his little gang often went to the State Hospital, for people who were mentally ill. When they saw some of the patients walking around, they would find a way to help them leave the grounds, under the fence, then return them back to the administrative office at the hospital where they would be rewarded with a dollar.

In 1951, Roberto was 13 years old. America was once again at war, this time on the Korean peninsula. His Uncle Arturo had been drafted and sent to Korea. Arturo, whom Roberto connected with more than anybody in his family, was the youngest of the first generation of the uncles and aunts. They had more of a brother-to-brother relationship than an uncle-to-nephew relationship. Arturo was Emilia's youngest child and Roberto's was Emilia's youngest grandchild so they naturally connected. He was Roberto's defender and protector. Roberto would do anything for his Uncle Arturo.

On March 31, 1951, Roberto was outside playing basketball. His sister Mariana came to bring him home. When Roberto saw her, Mariana was crying. He knew something was wrong. When he neared the house, there were a couple of cars parked by the house. Roberto heard Emilia screaming and wailing in Spanish. He just knew that his uncle had been killed in Korea.

The next day, Roberto went on his paper route, carrying the 200 or so newspapers with his uncle's picture on the front page, the front-page story of the local hero killed in Korea.

It was difficult for Roberto to see his beloved Emilia in pain. She spent hours staring out the window, tears streaming down her face. He just could not cope with her suffering. He began thinking of getting out of the house.

Recruiters from far off farmlands came to the Las Vegas barrio in big trucks hooked up with microphones, announcing that money could be made in Colorado. These recruiters set up a booth in the park and people signed up. Roberto learned that one of his best friends, Antonio Monroe and his family, were leaving to work in the migrant stream in Colorado.

Roberto was approaching his 14th birthday. He didn't have the nerve to ask his grandparents to let him go but told Antonio's family he had their permission. He was afraid that if he did ask, they would say no. Roberto secretly packed a bag and left with the Monroe family on a train to Pueblo, Colorado where they were picked up by a truck and transported to a big ranch. He made arrangements for a friend to tell his grandparents after he left.

Roberto and the Monroe family followed the migrant stream in search of work. Their search led them to fields in other parts of Colorado, Kansas, and Wyoming. On that first day in the field outside of Pueblo, the foreman gave Roberto a short hoe and pointed him toward endless rows of beets, three or four inches high. He spent the day in the blistering sun, stooped over, thinning the rows of beets. The temperature in the fields often rose to 115 degrees. He was sweating to earn his pay of 60 cents an hour.

One day, he noticed a group of white boys working in an adjoining field with long hoes. Having a long hoe meant not having a stoop down. Roberto went over to the white boys and found out that they were being paid 70 cents an hour. He immediately confronted the foreman to find out why the white boys were being paid more. The foreman asked Roberto if he were a communist and told him to go back to work or he would be fired.

Roberto went back to work.

Roberto, Billy Frank Jr., and Stella. Photo courtesy El Centro de la Raza

CHAPTER 9: On His Own

After the summer of 1954, Roberto and the Monroe family parted ways. The Monroe family returned to New Mexico while Roberto headed north. He had learned that his aunt had a friend who lived in Seattle so decided to give the Pacific Northwest a try. Roberto wrote to tell his aunt's friend that he was coming. He was almost fifteen and had been out on his own for a year.

Roberto knew very little about Seattle. He knew it rained a lot there. He also knew that Seattle had a baseball team, the Rainiers, who played in the Pacific Coast Baseball League. It was a typical cloudy September day on Roberto's first day in Seattle. His aunt's friend and her family lived in Georgetown. The first thing that Roberto wanted to do in Seattle, he told the sons of his aunt's friend, was to see Sick's Seattle Stadium, the baseball stadium where the Seattle Rainiers played.

They started walking from Georgetown toward the baseball stadium. On the way, through Beacon Hill, Roberto passed by Beacon Hill Elementary School. Some boys were playing basketball on the school playfield. Roberto and his friends challenged one group of boys and played basketball for an hour or so. (Years later, the old Beacon Hill Elementary School would become the home of El Centro de la Raza, the agency Roberto was instrumental in establishing.)

Later that afternoon, Roberto saw his first baseball game played in a real baseball stadium.

For Roberto, the move to Seattle was an exciting adventure. It was dramatically different than living in New Mexico. In New Mexico, it was green during the spring and early summer but completely barren and brown in the fall and winter. In Seattle, it was green all the time. And there was the water. Roberto had loved being near water. He marveled at the rivers and huge lakes that surrounded Seattle.

Roberto enrolled in school and his first day, at Cleveland High School, in the fall of 1954, exposed him to an entire new world. Being of the age where girls were becoming increasingly significant, Roberto was amazed at the many different girls he encountered for the first time-- Black girls, white girls, Asian girls, and a sprinkling of Indian girls.

Larry, Roberto, and Eddie Rye (far right) Jr. circa early 1970s. Photo courtesy El Centro de la Raza

He was amazed that there were no Chicano girls or boys. Roberto was perhaps the second or third Chicano student who had ever gone to Cleveland. He stuck out. Other students constantly asked him to say something in Spanish. He played along, often swearing in Spanish, knowing that the others wouldn't know what he really said.

One person at Cleveland High School did know Spanish--the Spanish teacher, Harrison Bailey. Even though Roberto was raised with a Spanish language background, he barely knew how to write or read in Spanish. Bailey had a great impact on young Roberto. He made Roberto feel that knowing the Spanish language was a valuable advantage. Roberto began to realize that Spanish was just as complicated, limitless, and sophisticated as any other language. Roberto loved going to school but due to unforeseen circumstances, ended up dropping out of school to find a job.

In 1958, Roberto learned that his brother Francisco had received a scholarship to Highlands University in Las Vegas, New Mexico.

From the time they were born, the Maestas brothers had a competitive relationship. Francisco often had the upper hand. When they were kids, Francisco rooted for the New York Yankees while Roberto rooted for the Boston Red Sox. In the years they were kids, the Yankees almost always won while the Red Sox never won the World Series.

Now, Francisco was a college man while Roberto, in comparison, was a high school dropout. The fact that his brother was going to college gave Roberto a renewed drive to obtain his high school diploma. Roberto believed that if Francisco could to go to college, so could he.

That fall, Roberto enrolled in an adult high school basic education program at the Edison Technical School. His grandparents had taught him the value of having an education but this wasn't high school. He found himself in a class of adults who, like him, had been unable to get a high school diploma. He had found an evening job at the Boeing Company that paid $1.32 an hour.

Roberto went to school all day, came home, got ready for work, went to work in the late afternoon, and got off at midnight. It became a daily grind but Roberto stuck it out. He was determined to get his high school diploma then go to college. He got his diploma and then applied to the UW. In the fall of 1959, Roberto entered the UW as a freshman.

College proved to be challenging for Roberto. He continued to work on the evening shift at the Boeing Company. Every morning, he got up, drove his raggedy car from South Park to the University campus, went to class, then back to South Park to change, then to work, worked his shift, then drove his raggedy car home where he studied at night. He scraped enough money to pay for tuition and textbooks.

Once, while studying with a classmate, Roberto went to a fraternity house on Greek row. His classmate pulled out a drawer from a file cabinet where the fraternity had dozens of samples of tests in any subject. He was impressed when he learned that the fraternity had staff that cooked meals for the fraternity members. That's when Roberto realized that the deck was stacked against him. The fraternity had resources with samples of tests and materials to help their members succeed. They had their meals cooked for them. They didn't have to work. Roberto realized that they weren't inherently smarter than him but he would have to work harder than them to succeed.

From his early days delivering the Las Vegas Daily Optic, Roberto had been a voracious reader. He learned a lot about world affairs, becoming very knowledgeable about a variety of political issues such as the Communist "Red Scare" phenomenon of the early fifties and the "military industrial complex." It was with great interest on New Year's Day in 1959 that Roberto followed the events taking place on the small island of Cuba. The Cuban military strongman, Fulgencio Batista, had fled the country in the face of a revolt.

Roberto sympathized with the Cuban people. The images of the Cuban people were very much like those of his aunts, neighbors, and elders of his little community back in New Mexico. Under Batista, Cuba had become a haven for American business and American gangsters. His regime took kickbacks. But the Cuban people didn't share in Batista's good fortune. They continued to live in poverty and those who opposed his rule were murdered or jailed. Roberto was thrilled when the people of Cuba overthrew their corrupt government.

Roberto eventually decided to become a teacher. Given his fluency in Spanish, Roberto felt there were more employment opportunities for a teacher with a foreign language background. He concentrated on his studies, taking the required number of courses toward earning a teaching certificate.

He graduated in 1965 from the UW. He was hired by the Seattle School District to teach Spanish at Franklin High School. It would later prove to be a significant turning point in Roberto's future.

The best to the very best. Thank you for making the world a better place and raising hell along the way

Ruthann Kurose,
Asian American Activist

LARRY GOSSETT
CHAPTER 10: Slavery, Segregation, and Education

Larry with other demonstrators at Seattle Central Community College 1972. Photo courtesy Gossett family

Growing up in Seattle's Central Area, Larry Gossett knew that one day he was going to be famous. He dreamed of being a professional sports star, either baseball or basketball. Indeed, he did become famous but not in the way he thought he would growing up.

His parents had come to Seattle to escape the blatant discrimination that existed in the South. Nelmon and Johnnie Gossett came north to Seattle from Texas in 1944. Both were descendants of slaves. Both were born in the 1920's and raised in small, rural Southern towns. Nelmon, the oldest of three, was born in Colorado City, Texas, the son of a janitor. Johnnie, the sixth of seven children, was born in Jacksonville, Texas, the daughter of the pastor of the local Colored Methodist Episcopal church.

Texas in the 1920s was a very racist living environment. Cotton was still king of the South and white cotton farmers were at the top of the power structure. Employment opportunities for African Americans were limited. Picking cotton was practically the only job available. For Nelmon Gossett, a full day's work meant picking 150 pounds of cotton for a $1.25.

While slavery had been abolished, the Southern hierarchy remained the same with whites controlling the political power structure and blacks relegated to inferior status. It was a time when whites called black men "boy" regardless of age. Five- and six year-old white kids were raised with the notion that it was acceptable to call a black janitor "boy." Lynching of black men for showing disrespect to whites was not uncommon.

It was at Texas College, in 1943, where Nelmon Gossett met Johnnie Carter. Nelmon was nineteen years old and Johnnie was eighteen years old. Back in those days, you didn't play around when you were a courting a pastor's daughter.

One year later, they were married. Nelmon and Johnnie wanted to start a family but Nelmon told Johnnie that they had to get out of the South to better their lives for themselves and their children.

World War II had resulted in a booming economy for Seattle and brought a huge influx of blacks, attracted by employment

Five- and six year-old white kids were raised with the notion that it was acceptable to call a black janitor "boy."

opportunities in war-related industries. Johnnie's oldest sister, Editha Anderson was living in Seattle with her husband. They wrote letters back home to Texas that there were good paying jobs for "Negroes" or "Colored" folks up in Seattle. That's how many black families came up to the northern cities. Usually one and two came up, found a job then sent back for their brothers, sisters, children, parents, or cousins. They called it one of America's great migrations. The booming wartime industries in the Northern industrial cities held promise for good paying jobs.

Johnnie had become pregnant and anything was better than a future of picking cotton, so Nelmon and Johnnie boarded a train in July of 1944 and went north. Eventually, three of Johnnie's four sisters and Nelmon's younger brother and sister migrated to Seattle and raised their families in the Pacific Northwest.

On February 21, 1945, in a segregated wing in Seattle's Broadway Hospital, Nelmon and Johnnie Gossett welcomed their first-born child, Edward Lawrence Gossett, into the world, later known as Larry. Larry entered the world in unexpected fashion. His mother had the urge to use the facilities but when she got on the toilet, Larry "popped out" into the toilet water. Fortunately, the umbilical cord did not break.

Johnnie screamed for her sister, Editha, and for a nurse on duty to no avail. Eventually, the nurse came running to the room. Exasperated, the nurse told Johnnie: "I'm tired of you colored girls having all these babies." Johnnie, who had never had a baby before, was insulted by the comment, but kept her mouth shut.

Nelmon, Larry's father, was not present for the birth. He had been sent home by the hospital administrators to get the funds to pay for the birth. They did not trust that Nelmon would pay his bill because he did not bring enough money to pay the entire hospital bill up front.

Larry's mother and father would later discover that no white couple having a baby at that hospital had ever been sent home for not paying their hospital bill up-front.

Nelmon and Johnnie would have five more children after Larry. There was Brenda (born February 3, 1947), Richard (born August 25, 1949), Glenn (born February 14, 1952), Theresa (born April 9, 1953), and Patrick (born November 1, 1955).

In Larry's High Point neighborhood of the late 1940s--early 1950s, black children and white children, had one thing in common. They were poor. Even though, as Larry recalled, that about one-third of the people in his High Point neighborhood were white, he had no white friends growing up. While the physical boundaries allowed blacks and whites to live in close proximity, the social boundaries that maintained their segregated worlds continued to exist.

Larry was always a hungry child. The Gossetts were poor but Larry didn't know it. Johnnie told her friends that her son Larry was 'the eat-inest child you ever saw.' He was always climbing on Johnnie's lap and asking her for something to eat. And he loved to play sports. Larry liked playing with any type of ball - basketballs, footballs, baseballs, and kickballs.

When Larry was eight years old in 1953, a little white boy in his High Point Elementary School called him a "nigger" because Larry's team beat the white boy's team in kickball. Larry knew that "nigger" was a hurtful word. It made him mad but didn't know why. Larry's parents didn't talk much about race. They had moved north to escape the racism of their upbringing.

When Larry was in the third grade, he told his teacher he wanted to be a baseball player or a lawyer. She told him that those jobs were not realistic occupations for 'Negroes.' Attitudes like hers and other white teachers sent the message to Larry and his black classmates that they were not as smart as the white kids. Negative expectations led to negative performance. As such, Larry considered himself to be an "average" student.

But when Larry had a black teacher, his fourth grade teacher Orie Green, she expected him to do as well, if not better, than the white kids in the classroom and he did. Orie Green was a remarkable woman. She was born with a congenital hip disability that kept her in casts and braces until she entered high school. When she applied for a job as a teacher, few school districts would hire a black teacher. Yet, she persisted and became one of the Seattle's first African American teachers in 1949.

Larry 1945 Seattle. Photo courtesy Gossett family

By 1955, Nelmon Gossett had saved enough money to buy a house. He wanted to live in West Seattle but was told that Negroes couldn't buy homes in West Seattle. For many years, there were few neighborhoods in Seattle, which allowed black families to live there. Racially restrictive covenants and housing discrimination effectively stamped many areas of the city as "Whites only" or "Negroes not allowed." Unscrupulous realtors made the argument that if non-whites moved into the neighborhood, property values would go down but the primary reason for these covenants was to keep the areas "White."

Neighborhoods like Capitol Hill, Mt. Baker, and Broadmoor remained closed not only to black families but to all families of color. One of the few neighborhoods open to black families was the Central Area. The Gossett family moved to 18th Avenue and Alder in the Central Area in the summer of 1955, right before Larry entered the fifth grade at Horace Mann Elementary School, a school where half the students were African American and all of the teachers were white.

CHAPTER 11: Nelmon: "Go To School"

As a youth, Larry was consumed with sports. Larry was a good athlete and the coaches liked him. He dreamed of going to college to play basketball. He thought as a player, he was good even though he was a skinny 5'7" 140 pounder. Larry became a regular at the Central Area Rotary Boy's Club, where he polished his skills playing basketball after school. During the 7th grade, Larry was so good at playing basketball, he became the only 7th grader and youngest member on the Boys Club varsity team, which had otherwise consisted of 9th graders.

When Larry was eleven, he made an all-star youth baseball team that went to Atlanta to play against some of the nation's best little league players.

While Larry was in the eighth grade at Washington Junior High School, he joined a street gang, the Junior Cobras. Every black kid had to join a gang. He thought it was a "cool thing" to do. He noticed the kind of respect that gang members got at Washington Junior High School. He was impressed with himself, a tough guy.

One day, the leader of the Junior Cobras told Larrry and the gang that they had to fight another gang, the "Cats" at Yesler Terrace. Larry thought that a fight meant throwing fists and punching someone. He was not prepared, especially when the Cats pulled out knives and razor blades. One of the Cats cut Larry on the chin, a scar that he carries to this day. The police siren blared and everyone ran. Larry was brought to Providence Hospital on 15th and Jefferson and got stitches on both sides of his chin. Nelmon Gossett was not happy with his son. He lectured his son, scolded him, and made it clear that Larry would have nothing further to do with the Junior Cobras.

In the summer of 1959, after Larry had finished the 8th grade, his father Nelmon announced to the family that they were moving to California. While Larry's brothers and sister were excited about the move, Larry didn't want to move. But when Nelmon told the family they were moving, Larry had no choice--they were moving.

The Gossett family settled in a home in a housing project in the Watts section of Los Angeles. Nelmon took a job at the post office. Larry was miserable. He felt intimidated by the other kids in the project. He complained to his parents that the other kids didn't get along with each other, that they were always fighting, and that they thought that beating other people was fun. He was scared.

Nelmon saved enough money to leave the housing project in Watts and bought a house in Compton, California in an all-black neighborhood. Larry was assigned to Walton Junior High School where he attended the 9th grade. He felt fortunate that he could play basketball, a skill, which gave him a small measure of respect from his peers.

But Larry was homesick and kept complaining to his mother and father. Finally, they had enough of Larry's complaining. After school was over in June of 1960, they put Larry on a Greyhound bus to Seattle and sent him to live with his aunt back in the Central Area.

In the fall of 1960, Larry entered Garfield High School, grateful to be back in Seattle. At that time, Garfield was perhaps the most integrated school in the entire state of Washington. Black students made up about one-third of the student population. Larry happily joined the basketball team as a tenth grader. Garfield was a mecca for black athletes.

In early 1961, Nelmon realized that living in California was not as good as he hoped for his family so the Gossetts returned to Seattle. Both Nelmon and Johnnie found work at the post office. They saved enough money to buy a house on Beacon Hill. Larry was happy to be back with his family but had to transfer from Garfield to Franklin High School.

When Larry entered Franklin in the fall of 1961, he found a school that was overwhelmingly white. There were only fifty black students. At Garfield, with its large black student population, Larry blended in, but at Franklin, Larry stood out. He felt very uncomfortable and his grades began to suffer. But he still had sports.

Larry became a starter on the school's basketball team in his senior year. The other four starters were also black. When Franklin played Garfield's basketball team who also started five black players, it was the first time in Seattle's high school sports history that 10 black players were on the same floor starting against each other. Both gyms were packed when the teams played each other with hundreds turned away. Larry enjoyed his status as a sports hero, a high school celebrity admired for his athleticism.

Larry Gossett wanted to play collegiate basketball. In the fall of 1962, as a senior in high school, he enrolled in college preparatory classes and did just enough school work to pass these courses. He didn't put a lot of effort in his academics, just enough to maintain his sports eligibility. As a 5' 8' point guard, the major colleges didn't recruit Larry. Larry's plan was to go to junior college and play basketball for two years, play well enough to get attention from the major colleges, then transfer to play ball for his junior and senior years. But his father Nelmon had other ideas.

Nelmon Gossett believed in a college education as a means of being successful in life. When Larry told his father he wanted to go to junior college to play ball, Nelmon said no. He told Larry that he would do anything to get Larry into the UW.

In the spring of 1963, true to his word, Nelmon Gossett set up an appointment and took his son to the UW Admissions Office. Larry didn't want to go but couldn't say no to his father. The Director of Admissions checked Larry's high school transcript and found that Larry needed to pass one semester of math to meet the minimum admissions requirements for UW. Larry didn't want to go to night school but Nelmon told Larry, that's what the man said, then that's what you are going to do. After being forced to finish one semester of geometry, Larry entered the UW as a freshman in the fall of 1963.

As Larry entered the UW, his life was going to be significantly changed. Basketball would lose its hold on him. Circumstances on campus, in the streets of Seattle, and in the nation overall would raise his political awareness and call for his involvement in the flourishing civil rights movement.

Circumstances on campus, in the streets of Seattle, and in the nation overall would raise his political awareness and call for his involvement in the flourishing civil rights movement.

Larry (with bow tie) and other kids in Central area neighborhood circa early 1950s. Photo courtesy Gossett family

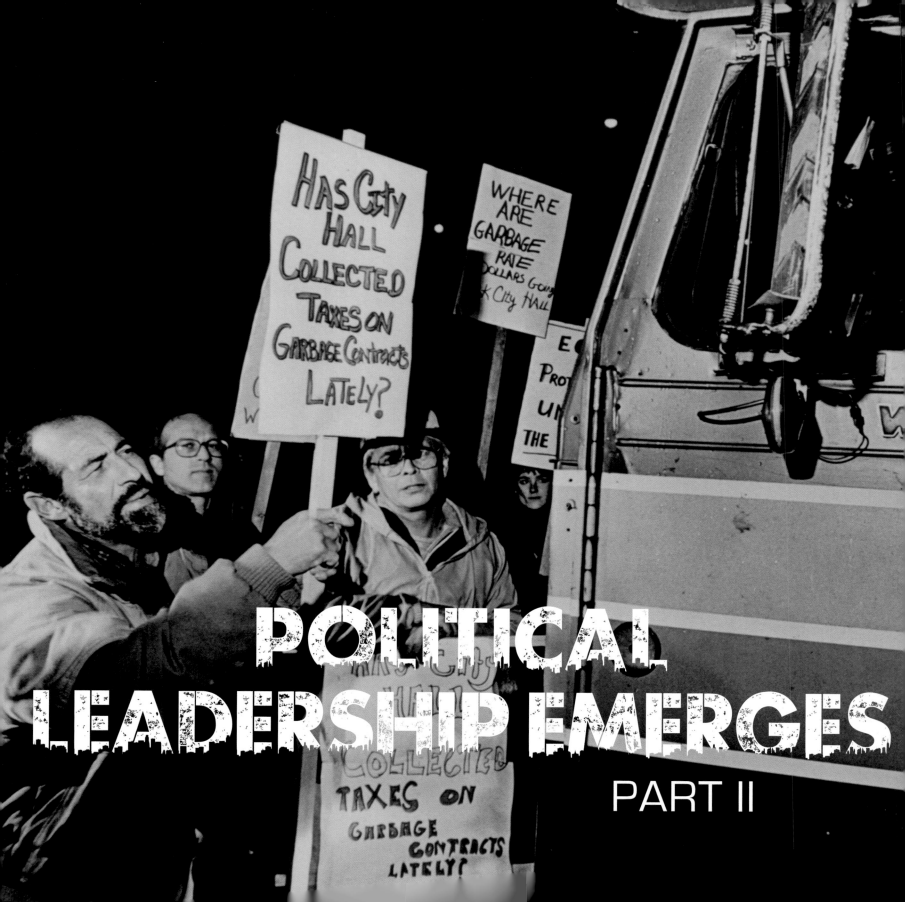

POLITICAL LEADERSHIP EMERGES

PART II

CHAPTER 12: The Nation Shakes

The 1960s saw the emergence of a national civil rights movement. Issues such as employment discrimination, open housing, segregated education, and voting rights were receiving increasing national and local attention. Civil rights protests, demonstrations, sit-ins and marches were growing in number.

Open or fair housing was of particular concern to Seattle's Black community. In the 1950 census, 69 percent of Seattle's Black population was found to have lived in the Central District. By 1960, that percent had grown to 78 percent. The implication was clear--Blacks couldn't find housing in other neighborhoods.

On June 15, 1963, Reverend Mance Jackson led a group of about 1,000 protesters from the Mt. Zion Baptist Church to Westlake Mall in support of open housing, the first significant civil rights march in Seattle.

On July 1, 1963, thirty-five protesters, organized by the Central District Youth Club held a sit-in, the first of its kind in Seattle, in Mayor Gordon S. Clinton's office to complain about the lack of progress the City government had made toward open housing. The sit-in lasted twenty-four hours. It ended after Mayor Clinton promised to form a human rights commission to write an open housing ordinance.

On July 25, 1963, the protesters again held a sit-in at the Mayor's office to complain about the racial composition of Mayor Clinton's newly formed Human Rights Commission. The mayor had appointed only two blacks to the Commission. The protesters demanded open housing immediately. This time, the sit-in lasted for four days. Twenty-two protesters were arrested in the first arrests of Seattle's civil rights movement. The Human Rights Commission did draft an open housing ordinance, making housing discrimination a misdemeanor.

But when submitted to the voters of Seattle in 1964, the open housing ordinance was defeated by a two-to-one margin.

On August 28, 1963, about 200,000 people joined the March on Washington. It was on that day when the Reverend Dr. Martin Luther King, Jr. delivered his famous "I Have a Dream" speech.

Meanwhile, Bob Santos was working at the Boeing Company, recovering from his financial disaster as a jazz concert promoter. Roberto Maestas was in college, earning credits toward a teaching degree. Larry Gossett was in summer school, preparing for college. Bernie Whitebear was undergoing a political epiphany, taking his first steps of political activism.

Roberto and Bob 1986. Photo courtesy Seattle Times

CHAPTER 13: Bernie, Buffalo Chips and Indian Fishing Rights

By 1963, Bernie, now known as Bernie Whitebear, was fully engaged in the Indian Fishing Rights Movement. During the years that he had spent in the military, the relationship between Native Americans and white sports fishermen had deteriorated to increasingly violent confrontations, especially at Frank's Landing on the Nisqually River. The white sports fisherman had the support of the State's Fish and Wildlife Commission. State authorities confiscated Native American fishing equipment and boats in a concentrated effort to blunt the growing Indian Fishing Rights Movement.

It was the position of the State's Fish and Wildlife Commission that Native Americans were restricted to fishing on their reservations. The Native American tribes, on the other hand, believed that treaty rights signed by their fore bearers with the white man's government gave them the right to fish, no matter where. The Nisqually, in particular, were particular insistent about their fishing rights. The U.S. Army had forced the Nisqually off their reservation to build a military base during World War II so they had no place to fish.

One day, Bernie showed up at Frank's Landing with a leather headband around his head to lend his support. He took off his pants and put on a self-made breechcloth. He put on an old pair of white sneakers with holes above the toes, found a bamboo pole to which he tied a white feather, and joined the small group of protesters. When confronted by the group, Bernie told them his name was Buffalo Chips, which brought smiles and laughter. He was welcomed by the group, especially with the cigarettes, food, and containers of hot coffee he brought for them to share.

The struggle at Frank's Landing brought national attention to the Indian Fishing Rights Movement. In 1964, movie icon Marlon Brando showed up to offer his celebrity in support of the cause. Brando held press conferences to highlight the struggle for equal fishing rights. The press obliged, taking pictures of Brando fishing for salmon alongside Bob Satiacum. Other celebrities such as Peter and Jane Fonda and Dick Gregory made trips to Frank's Landing, bringing the press with them.

Bernie was concerned that urban Native Americans, particularly the youth, were in danger of losing touch with their heritage and culture. He began working with various Native American youth groups, organizing traditional dancing, drumming, and singing activities. He brought in Plains and Plateau Native American elders to share their wisdom and expertise with the youth. Bernie sponsored pow wows at the Masonic Temple in Seattle to give the youth some exposure to these traditional Native American arts.

Bernie had always been musically inclined. As a child, he learned to play the trumpet by memory and eventually learned to read music. He was the lead trumpet in his high school band. He enjoyed performing and even joined a Boeing employee group of entertainers, performing as Sitting Bull in a stage production of "Annie Get Your Gun."

In 1968, Bernie was invited to join the Koleda Dance Ensemble, a Balkan dance folk group, on a three-month tour to Europe. Bernie raised enough money to bring a small group of youth on the trip. They traveled to Europe where they performed in Germany, France, Greece, and Turkey. Bernie found that Europeans were very curious about Native Americans. Wherever they went, the press wanted interviews. Bernie came to the conclusion that Europeans were more sensitive to Native Americans than Americans because in America, Native Americans were ignored.

Returning home, Bernie decided to take action. There were no federal, state, county, or city funds available for services to the estimated 25,000 Native Americans in Seattle. The American Indian Women's Service League provided limited help but existed on donations and volunteers. Bernie volunteered with a free clinic, operating three nights a week, for Native Americans, which had been organized by Alaskan Native Bob Lupson at the Marine Public Health Hospital on Seattle's Beacon Hill.

In 1969, the clinic became known formally as the Seattle Indian Health Board and was established as a non-profit organization. Bernie quit his job at Boeing to become the first Executive Director of the agency.

> Wherever you go in Indian Country, there is always one name that is remembered, Bernie Whitebear.

Ralph Forquera,
Seattle Indian Health Board

CHAPTER 14: Bob Holding Up The Banner

In the mid-1960s, Bob Santos was firmly rooted in the role of family man. He and his wife Anita had saved enough money from their jobs at the Boeing Company to buy their first house, a small two-bedroom rambler, which overlooked Sick's Stadium in the Mt. Baker neighborhood. Bob and Anita began raising a family, eventually having six children-- Danny, Simone, Robin, Tom, John, and Nancy -- three sons and three daughters. They quickly outgrew their first house and moved into Anita's childhood home in the Rainier Valley. They would eventually put a down payment on a seven-bedroom home near Columbia City in South Seattle.

But while Bob's home life was progressing nicely, he wasn't satisfied with the direction his professional life was going. Always the risk taker, Bob left the Boeing Company to sell insurance for the Knights of Columbus.

In 1964, Bob met Walter Hubbard, then president of the local Catholic Interracial Council (CIC), who convinced Bob to participate in a march in support of open housing. Bob had never been involved in political demonstrations before. He ended up joining his fellow marchers at St. James Cathedral, where he was handed a pole that held the CIC banner. It rained that day, with winds battering the banner that Bob clutched. He was determined to hold the banner against the blustery winds, knowing that he couldn't let the banner hit the ground. The weather was so miserable that Bob told himself that this was the last march he would ever participate in!

However the next morning, Bob's picture appeared on the front page of the Catholic newspaper, with him valiantly holding the banner. Friends called Bob to relay their admiration for his "brave" political stand. After a few words of encouragement, Bob decided that participating in a march for a good cause wasn't so bad after all.

From that point on, Bob considered himself a civil rights activist.

Bob became more involved in the local civil rights movement. The Catholic Interracial Council took progressive stands in support of open housing, equal employment, school desegregation, and the banning of Class H liquor licenses to private clubs, which excluded non-whites from joining. When the Catholic Interracial Council took a stand, supporting the United Farm Workers boycott of lettuce at Safeway, Bob took his turn, joining marches and sit-ins.

In 1966, Bob was elected President of the Catholic Interracial Council to replace Walter Hubbard who had left the Council to become the Executive Director of the newly formed CARITAS (Community Action, Remedial Instruction, Tutorial, and Assistance Service) Program, a program designed to help inner-city youth. Soon, Bob was being recognized as an up and coming civil rights leader. In 1969, he was appointed by Seattle Mayor Floyd Miller to serve on the newly formed Seattle Human Rights Commission.

Bob circa 1965. Photo courtesy Santos family

Bob with protestors John Spellman's office 1973 (seated left Rhonda Gossett"). Photo courtesy INTER*IM

Bob and son Danny South African Consulate 1985. Photo by Dean Wong

CHAPTER 15: Black Power

In 1964, Larry Gossett was one of only 40 black students in a sea of white students on the UW campus. He was still preoccupied with sports. Most of his friends, such as Levi Fisher, Tom Greenlee, Bob Flowers, Al Roberts, and David Carr, were athletes and on scholarship. Larry was determined to play college basketball but the basketball coach told Larry he was too small and discouraged him from trying out.

As a college freshman, Larry was afraid to speak up in class because of a belief that he wasn't as articulate or intellectual as the white students. Since Nelmon had paid for Larry's tuition, Larry felt that he owed it to his father to stick it out. Larry's grades were about average, so he felt enough confidence to continue and committed himself to graduating from college.

Politics was not yet in Larry's realm of consciousness but he was aware of the civil rights movement. As a college student, Larry kept up with the issues of the day--the issue of civil rights was often a topic of discussion. In February of 1965, Malcolm X was murdered in New York City. Malcolm X scared Larry because he talked about the need for black people to pick up guns and rise against their oppressors. At the time, Larry thought this was counterproductive. He favored the non-violent teachings of the Reverend Martin Luther King, Jr.

The war in Vietnam was beginning to escalate. Larry didn't think too much about the social or political implications of the war but he didn't want to be drafted. He began exploring alternatives to the draft, seeking a legitimate deferment, and met a recruiter for the VISTA (Volunteers in Service to America) Program. He applied, was accepted, and entered the VISTA Program in the spring of 1966 and was sent to training in Toledo, Ohio for VISTA volunteers.

Larry was beginning to be exposed to books and radical thought that he never experienced at the UW. He read such books as "Rules for Radicals," a primer on grassroots organizing, written by Saul Alinsky, (often called the father of modern American radicalism) and "The Other America," a groundbreaking study on poverty written by Michael Harrington, one of the leaders of the Socialist Party. The VISTA training Larry participated in gave him a new perspective on his view of the world.

After his training in Toledo, Larry was assigned to work in New York City, first in a neighborhood on the lower east side in black and Puerto Rican neighborhoods and then eventually in Harlem, a community of a half million people, almost all black with a sprinkling of Puerto Ricans.

One of his first duties was to complete a needs survey, in which he found that 9,000 people lived on 11th Street, on the block where he was assigned to provide services. Back in Seattle, by comparison, there were 110 people on the block he grew up on. Larry had never seen so many people packed in such a small space! Indeed, the poverty and overcrowding he witnessed had a profound impact.

Larry was put in charge of a youth program in Harlem, providing tutoring and recreational activities to children under the age of 12. Although Larry had lived in a public housing project in Seattle, it was nothing like the living conditions these children were forced to endure. There were rats and roaches everywhere, junkies and drunks passed out on the sidewalks, dilapidated housing, overcrowding: a community which lacked hope and no control of its destiny.

It became very easy for Larry to understand why people, forced to live in such conditions, would turn to alcohol or drugs to escape. And this was New York City, the so-called greatest city in the world, with its tall Manhattan skyscrapers, its bright Broadway neon lights, and its rich Wall Street financial dealings. Larry found the contrasting situations steeped in hypocrisy and contradictions.

One month after Larry started working in New York, two men from the Student Non-Violent Coordinating Committee, Stokely Carmichael and Willie Ricks, came to speak at an event. They raised the issue of "Black Power," the concept of black people controlling their own destiny, their own economy, without having to rely on the white man.

Larry was intrigued. He immersed himself in soaking up what, for him, were new ideas. He read materials about or written by Lenin, Karl Marx, and Che Guevara. He learned about Martin L. Delany and Marcus Garvey, black separatists of the 19th Century.

He began to accept the philosophy advanced by Malcolm X and attended meetings of the Organization of African American Unity, founded by Malcolm X, designed to fight for social and economic justice.

The radicalization of Larry Gossett was dramatic and deep. He grew a "natural." He started wearing "shades." He wore dashikis every day. He took the Muslim name of "Mohamed Aba Yoruba."

In 1967, when Larry's VISTA service was completed, he thought about remaining in New York, but decided to return to Seattle, where he felt he could bring the lessons about Black Power that he learned in Harlem back to make a difference in the black community. He had discovered the value of community organizing.

When Larry returned to Seattle in the fall of 1967, he found a much different black community than the one he had left.

Earlier that year, April 19, 1967, Stokely Carmichael came to Seattle and spoke to an overflowing crowd of 2,000 at Garfield High School. Carmichael inspired his audience to take up the cause of "Black Power." People who had called themselves "Negroes" before Carmichael's speech were calling themselves "Black" after the speech. Young local black activists such as Sadikifu Akina-James and the Dixon brothers, Elmer and Aaron, emerged and formed a Seattle chapter of the Student Non-Violent Coordinating Committee. Larry joined the group and reentered the UW.

On the Thanksgiving Day weekend of 1967, Larry and 32 other young black activists went to Los Angeles to participate in the first West Coast Black Power Youth Conference. This conference brought approximately 400 politically black high school-aged and college-aged youth from throughout the West Coast to learn about "Black Power" from such newly formed national groups as the BSU, the United Slaves, and the Black Panther Party and from such Black Power advocates as James Forman, Stokely Carmichael, and H. Rap Brown. It was an attempt to create a national movement of black activists in search of self-determination. Speaker after speaker urged the audience to be proud of their blackness and to be involved in seizing power to control their own destinies.

When Larry and the other Seattle activists returned to Seattle, they decided to disband the local chapter of the Student Non-Violent Coordinating Committee and on January 8, 1968, formed a BSU at the UW. Larry was elected to coordinate organizing efforts in Washington and Oregon with the goal of organizing BSUs in middle schools, high schools, and colleges throughout Washington-Oregon area.

Larry became a local spokesman for "Black Power." In a December 27, 1967 interview with Hilda Bryant of the Seattle Post Intelligencer, Larry stated, "I believe that black people must be obsessed with thinking black. Then they will understand the need for determining their own destiny."

He added that blacks should have the same amount of power that reflects their numbers in the community, stating, "If there are thirty-percent black people they should be represented by thirty-percent of the decision-makers."

When asked to define "Black Power," Larry replied, "Black Power" means "self determination, self-respect, self defense, and power by any means necessary."

By March of 1968, 27 BSUs were formed in Washington and Oregon. The primary focus of the BSU was to make the traditional educational system more accountable to black people.

For example, there were 2,416 classes at the UW but no class that addressed the black communities or other minority communities, i.e., the Third World communities. Larry and the other members of the University's BSU concluded that the institution was racist, that the curriculum needed to be integrated, and that there was a need to recruit more black and other minority students to the University. They decided to act now rather than later.

During the winter quarter of 1968, Larry and other members of the UW's BSU, such as Eddie Demmings, Garry Owens, and Tony Buford, started attending history classes at the University, challenging history professors to talk about "colonial" people and demanding that such courses include a black person's perspective. While some white students clapped, most sat in stunned silence.

Black students throughout the country were becoming more militant. Confrontations between black students and university administrators had grown as Black Power advocates demanded an education more accountable to black Americans. Civil rights protests and demonstrations were frequently in the headlines. There had been riots in Newark, Detroit, and Los Angeles.

On the morning of March 29, 1968, Larry was in the office of the BSU when a phone call came in from a group of angry black students at Franklin High School. Two black female students had been sent home and told to straighten their Afro hairstyles. In addition, according to newspaper accounts, two black male students had been suspended the day before after a hallway scuffle with a white student. One of the students was placed on a home suspension but allowed to come back on the following Monday. The other had been placed on an indefinite suspension. The Principal had refused to rescind the suspensions.

The black students at Franklin wanted to burn the school down. Larry convinced the group to meet with him before taking any action.

Larry, along with fellow BSU members Aaron Dixon and Carl Miller, drove immediately to Franklin High School and met with about 150 students. Together, the group drew up a list of demands to present to Franklin High School's administration. These demands included a reinstatement of the students who had been suspended, the inclusion of an Afro-American history class, the placement of portraits of notable Black Americans on the school walls, recognition of the BSU, and the hiring of a black principal or vice principal.

At approximately 12:30 that afternoon, the group of 150 or so walked across the street to the school, chanting "Beep, Beep, Bang, Bang, Ungowa, Black Power." They walked into the Principal's office. The demonstrators crammed into the 16-foot by 16-foot office space. The protesters announced that they wouldn't leave until School Superintendent Forbes Bottomly responded to their demands.

The situation was tense. Classes were cancelled. Students were sent home. The Seattle Police Department was called and a sizable force of police gathered at the parking lot of nearby Sick's Seattle Stadium awaiting orders to storm the school and put down the demonstration.

Larry with protesters Franklin High School sit-in 1968. Photo courtesy CAMP

CHAPTER 16: Demands and Jail

As the drama unfolded, Loren Ralph, the Principal, called Superintendent Bottomly. School officials called mediators. Officials from the Central Area Motivation Program, including Vince Hayes, Bob Flowers, and Tom Givan, and the City's Human Rights Commission such as Phil Hayasaka and John Eichelberger, came to Franklin to speak to the protesters. The mediators convinced the group to leave the school administration area and go to the school auditorium for a discussion of the group's demands.

Eventually, the Principal agreed to meet with the students at the Seattle Human Rights Commission office on the following Monday to discuss the suspensions and group's demands.

On Monday, April 1, 1968, the main story of the day was the announcement that President Lyndon Johnson would not run for re-election. Elsewhere, racial tensions in Memphis, Tennessee over a garbage strike were becoming heated. The Reverend Martin Luther King, Jr. announced that he was postponing a trip to Kenya to go to Memphis instead to intervene.

On April 1, 1968, after a five hour hearing, the Seattle Human Rights Commission ruled that the suspended student be reinstated to Franklin High School. The panel of Human Rights Commissioners, chaired by Ben Woo, found discrepancies in testimony.

Woo, speaking for the panel, stated, "A fight which led to the suspension did not, in fact, occur." The Human Rights Commission also issued a set of recommendations including a review of district suspension procedures, improved communications between students and school administrators, and the establishment of student human relations committees or clubs.

Superintendent Bottomly issued a statement indicating that although he was disappointed at the Commission's findings and recommendations, he would follow the Commission's decision. He also vowed that those involved in the Franklin sit-in would be disciplined and urged the prosecutor's office to take legal action. Nine students were subsequently suspended for their role in the sit-in.

On the morning of April 4, 1968, the police arrested Carl Miller, Trolice Flavors, Aaron Dixon, and Ricki Gossett on the charge of unlawful assembly. Later that afternoon, Larry Gossett was also arrested on the charge of unlawful assembly. Ricki Gossett, Larry's brother, a postal worker, wasn't even at the Franklin sit-in. He was arrested because he was Larry's brother. Charges against Ricki Gossett were later dropped.

Larry, Carl Miller, and Aaron Dixon were in their jail cells on April 4, 1968 when the news came over the radio that the Reverend Martin Luther King, Jr. had been assassinated in Memphis. Cities across the nation were besieged with riots and angry mobs. Locally, police were called to deal with reports of property destruction, looting, and fire bombing in the Central Area and Rainier Valley.

And in the King County Jail, the black prisoners wanted to take their anger and frustration out on the white prisoners. Larry and his fellow Black Student Union members urged caution. They reminded the black inmates that Dr. King stood for nonviolence and that to take violent action was disrespectful of the principles that Dr. King stood for. They conducted an impromptu teach-in, enlightening their brethren that it was not "Black Power" to beat up powerless white prisoners.

The next day, Larry, Carl Miller, Aaron Dixon, and Trolice Flavors were led out of the jail cells in handcuffs, shackled with chains around their ankles, waist and hands for their arraignment.

The symbolism was obvious to Larry. He felt like a slave, he recalled. A crowd of over 1,000 had gathered at the courthouse for the arraignment. The halls and the courtroom were filled with family, friends, and supporters. Many spoke on behalf of the men, attesting to their good character. The prosecutor requested a bail of $1,500. The judge denied that request and to the cheers of the supporters, released each of the men on their personal recognizance.

Outside of the courtroom, Nelmon and Johnnie Gossett were concerned. They conveyed to Larry their experiences of the South with the accompanying violence that occurred to civil rights demonstrators. They were scared and asked Larry to stop his activism because they believed that he would be killed, hurt or jailed.

But Larry told his parents that he couldn't stop. He felt that after his VISTA experience, he had a special calling to serve and help black and other oppressed people in this racist capitalist society. The subject was never brought up again.

Energized by their success at Franklin High School, Larry Gossett and the BSU turned their attention to the UW.

In January of 1968, the BSU presented a list of demands to Dr. Charles Odegaard, president of the UW:

1. *Recruitment of more Black, Asian, Latino, Native American and poor Whites into the UW under flexible admissions criteria;*
2. *Establishment of a Black studies program;*
3. *Recruitment of more Black faculty, administrators, and counselors;*
4. *Establishment of social and cultural support systems for the students on campus;*
5. *That Black students be represented on advisory and decision-making bodies at the UW campus.*

The BSU set a deadline of May 19, 1968 for the demands to be met. May 19th was University Day. The date had special significance in 1968 because it marked the 100th Anniversary of the UW and it was anticipated that the Governor would be present. The plan was to stage a sit-in at the Administration Office and hold the Governor and President Odegaard hostage until the demands were met.

On May 20, 1968, the UW BSU sent out a call to the other BSUs, which had been formed at the local high schools. Approximately 150 or so black students and community members marched to the Administration Building at the University.

The group walked in, shouting "Equality Now!," on a meeting President Odegaard had with the Faculty Senate. E.J. Brisker once again presented the list of five demands, which the BSU had pressed.

After four hours of negotiations, President Odegaard agreed to all of the demands. The University would make a conscious effort to increase black enrollment, provide financial support to minority students, recruit minority staff and create a black studies program.

Larry received a great deal of media notoriety. He gave an interview to Seattle Magazine about his perspectives on the growing black power movement.

Larry said, "In general, the Black Student Union is a political organization set up to serve the wants and needs of black students on white campuses. The educational system is geared for white, middle class kids, so it has never served black students. We're educated to fit into some non-existent slot in white society, rather than be responsible to the needs of our own brothers in the ghetto. To combat this, one thing we want to do is establish courses in Afro-American culture and history."

No arrests were made as the result of the sit-in at the University. City officials were upset, determined to make an example of Larry and the BSU. Less than one month later, Gossett, Miller, Dixon, and Trolice Flavors went on trial for the earlier charges brought after the sit-in at Franklin High School.

On June 19, 1968, an all-white jury found the men guilty. The trial lasted six days but when the jury retired to the jury room, they returned in less than seven minutes, making this the shortest trial in the history of King County that ended in a guilty verdict.

The verdict touched off street violence in the Central Area that raged throughout the summer.

CHAPTER 17: Roberto - Teacher to Activist

One interested observer of the tense situation and sit-in at Franklin High School was young teacher Roberto Maestas. He had graduated from UW and was hired by the Seattle School District to teach at Franklin High School in the fall of 1966. Maestas felt a close affinity to students of color. He found that the darker the kids were, the farther they sat in the back of the room. He would make a special effort to reach out to them. When the black students took over the Principal's office, the staff were told to leave the building, but Maestas stayed to see how the drama played itself out. In fact, Maestas was the only teacher who stayed. He made it a point to talk with Larry Gossett and the others to understand why they took over the Principal's office. It was the first time Maestas crossed paths with Larry Gossett.

The sit-in at Franklin High School made Roberto Maestas ponder. The BSU demands for an African-American Studies course at Franklin resonated with Roberto. Up to then, Roberto had not considered himself to be very political. He agreed that there had been contributions which minorities made to society that were not taught in the history curriculum in public schools. He decided that he needed to learn the history of his own people.

In the summer of 1968, Roberto was teaching minority high school students in an Upward Bound program in Bellingham, Washington. Two of the students who came to his class daily were Laura McCloud and Allison Bridges, Native American teenage girls from the Nisqually Delta. They told Roberto and their classmates about the struggle for Indian fishing rights in the delta.

Roberto was fascinated by the determination of these two young women. They spoke of their need to fish, their right to fish, getting harassed by law enforcement, getting threatened by the white sports fishermen, getting arrested, and going to jail for something to believe in.

He made it a point to talk with Larry Gossett and the others to understand why they took over the principal's office. It was the first time Maestas crossed paths with Larry Gossett.

Roberto found out that Alison's father, Al Bridges, was one of the leaders of this movement. Roberto had to meet him and wanted to learn about the Indian Fishing Rights Movement. He invited himself to Alison's home over the Fourth of July weekend and introduced himself to Al Bridges. Bridges took Roberto to Frank's Landing to see for himself the ongoing conflicts between the Native Americans and white sports fishermen.

Over the next year, the political awakening of Roberto Maestas continued. In the course of his self-exploration, Roberto met and developed a relationship with Joseph Summers, a professor at UW, who taught literature about the Mexican revolution. Summers encouraged Roberto to become involved in Latino issues, arranging for Roberto to attend a Latino education conference in Monterey, California in the summer of 1969. This exposure to other Latinos discussing social, political, and educational issues only increased Roberto's desire to learn about his culture.

Summers arranged a fellowship for Roberto to attend graduate school to further his studies. Roberto would not return to Franklin and in the fall of 1969, Roberto enrolled at UW to obtain his Master's degree.

Just one year before Roberto entered UW, Larry Gossett and Carl Miller had gone to the Yakima Valley to recruit Chicano students for the university. When the two young black men showed up in the Valley, their presence was immediately known and viewed with distrust by the Chicano youth they sought out.

These Chicano youth, such as a young Jesus Sanchez, were ready to jump these two black guys from the city but decided to hear what Larry and Carl had to say. What they heard was intriguing. A college education had never been considered seriously by any of them before. And what they heard from two black men struck a cord. Some of these Chicano youth took up the offer of a college education.

Many of these Chicano youth had been active with the United Farm Workers, which had been organizing Yakima Valley farm workers since 1966. Immediately upon setting foot on campus, these Chicano students, led by Jose Correa, Antonio Salazar, Eron Maltos, Jesus Lemos, Erasmo Gamboa, and Eloy Apodaca, among many others, formed the United American Mexican students.

In a short time, the United American Mexican Students worked to establish a Mexican American Studies Program through the University's College of Arts and Science Department. Supported by other student groups, including the BSU, the United American Mexican Students organized a boycott of non-union grapes. The boycott led to a decision reached on February 19, 1969 that UW would no longer buy non-union grapes, making UW the first college to remove non-union grapes from its eating facilities.

When Roberto arrived on campus, the United American Mexican Students group was going through significant change. Many, if not all, of its members, including Roberto, rejected the term "Mexican American," arguing that the term, "Chicano" was more appropriate, in reflecting the growing ethnic consciousness of its members. Thus, MEChA (Movimiento Estudiantil Chicano de Aztlán, Chicano Student Movement of Aztlán) was created. Roberto joined his compadres in demanding more opportunities for Chicano students on campus and supporting farm worker rights off campus.

Roberto's campus activism allowed him to renew an acquaintance with Larry Gossett. Gossett remembered Maestas from the occupation of the Principal's office at Franklin. Maestas had been the only teacher at Franklin who had taken the time to talk with him and the other members of BSU who had led the occupation. The teacher was now a fellow activist.

Larry, Stella, and Roberto early 1970s at El Centro de la Raza.
Photo courtesy El Centro de la Raza

The boycott led to a decision reached on February 19, 1969 that UW would no longer buy non-union grapes, making UW the first college to remove non-union grapes from its eating facilities.

PATHS CROSS
PART III

CHAPTER 18 - Early Beginnings

In 1970, Bob Santos' mentor, Walter Hubbard left his job as Director of CARITAS to join the newly formed King County Office for Civil Rights. And just like before, Bob was asked to replace Hubbard, to take over the directorship of CARITAS. CARITAS was housed at St. Peter Claver Center, across from the Providence Hospital, right in the heart of the Central Area.

The St. Peter Claver Center served as a small center for community groups with office space and an auditorium. The Catholic Archdiocese operated the St. Peter Claver Center, named for a Jesuit priest who ministered to the poor in the Caribbean and the West Indies. Father Harvey McIntyre, the pastor of the nearby Immaculate Conception Church, was the caretaker for the building. Because of the heavy workload at the Church, Father McIntyre asked Bob to manage the building. It was Bob who had the responsibility of opening the building for community groups to use.

The early 1970s was a period of time when the anti-war movement, women's movement, civil rights movement, and labor movement took root in Seattle. In 1970, the St. Peter Claver Center was the local center of progressive activity. Many groups met there. The social hall at the Center was provided at no cost to several organizations, including the Black Panthers, which used it daily for their free breakfast program.

The Marion Club, a group of older Catholic women; the Blackfeet Indians of Montana, for tribal members in the Seattle area; the Coalition Against Discrimination; the Asian Coalition for Equality; the United Farm Workers, and Radical Women held their meetings there, as did the Central Contractors Association.

For many of these groups, St. Peter Claver Center was the only place in the area where they could hold meetings.

The Native American groups regularly opened their meetings with traditional drumming and ceremonial burning of sage. After one such meeting, one of the young Maryknoll sisters who lived in the convent next door ran up to Bob Santos.

She exclaimed, "Uncle Bob, those Indian kids are starting to smoke the sage!"

Bob replied, "It's okay as long as they don't inhale."

The nun didn't think it was funny and walked away, shaking her head. Complaints were made to the Catholic Archdiocese that the Center had been taken over by the "left wing."

The book The Gang of Four, follows the careers of Larry Gossett, Bob Santos, the late Roberto Maestas and the late Bernie Whitebear in the Pacific Northwest. The book will leave a lasting legacy for the many hundreds of students mentored by these four civil rights leaders. With even more enlightened students and activists to follow.

Apl.de.ap
Black Eyed Peas

The Apl.de.ap Foundation International promotes empowerment through education on a global scale.

Chapter 19: Tyree Scott and United Construction Workers Association

Meanwhile, an African American labor leader named Tyree Scott operated Scott's Electric, a minority electrician company. But Tyree had not been able to find a job. Minority contractors were being locked out of jobs. Trade unions excluded non-whites from joining. Tyree and about 60 other minority contractors organized in the spring of 1968 and formed the Central Contractors Association. Tyree was the chair and became the first President of the Central Contractors Association.

In 1969, funding provided by the Seattle Model Cities Program provided new opportunities for work on major public works projects. But minority contractors were still shut out from getting work. In response, Tyree and his supporters 'took to the streets.' Scott led demonstrations and marches to every federally-funded construction site, effectively shutting down work at Harborview Medical Center, the King County Administration Building, and the UW.

Tyree brought 100 or so demonstrators to shut down a job site at the Medgar Evers pool. This was the demonstration that brought Larry Gossett to the cause. Larry was upset that a construction job in the Central Area had only whites working at the job site. At the time, he was President of BSU at UW. The BSU was trying to find issues to connect students on campus with the community. Larry believed that involvement in Tyree's cause was a timely issue for students to identify with.

Tyree's cause also caught the attention of other civil rights organizations like the Catholic Interracial Council and the American Friends Service Committee. On November 6, 1969, Tyree and his supporters shut down construction work at Sea-Tac Airport. Forty eight protesters were cited for trespassing, including Tyree Scott, Father Michael Holland of St. Mary's church, representing the Catholic Interracial Council, and Dolores Sibonga, a future city councilwoman. As a result of the demonstrations, a class action civil rights lawsuit, U.S. vs. Ironworkers Local 86, was filed by the U.S. Department of Justice in 1969 against the building trade unions.

In 1969, internal conflicts within the Central Contractors Association about its direction caused Tyree to leave. Some in the Central Contractors Association wanted to concentrate primarily on the interests of the contractors. Tyree wanted equal focus on the workers. He was forced out.

With funding provided by the American Friends Service Committee, the United Construction Workers Association (UCWA) was formed. Tyree Scott was approached and he accepted the position of Executive Director with office space provided in the St. Peter Claver Center.

On June 16, 1970, Federal District Court Judge William Lindberg issued his decision in U.S. v. Ironworkers Local 86, ruling that Seattle's building trade union hiring practices and apprenticeship programs had discriminated against minority workers in violation of Title VII of the 1964 Civil Rights Act. Judge Lindberg ordered a broad affirmative action program for minority workers in the construction industry to be implemented through the Court Order Advisory Committee (COAC), a board representing all the parties in the dispute. It was a huge victory for Tyree Scott and UCWA.

In the summer of 1972, UCWA led dramatic protests that closed down Interstate 90, Seattle Central Community College, and other construction sites around the area. It had been almost two years since Judge Lindberg made his ruling, mandating the creation of an affirmative action program for minority workers in the building trades union, without any significant progress made. This affirmative action program was supposed to be implemented by the Court Order Advisory Committee that Judge Lindberg had created, with representatives from the building trades unions. But the building trades union representatives had voted to exclude Tyree Scott and UCWA from participation.

Tyree Scott and Bob at Seattle Central Community College being taken away by Seattle Police. Photo courtesy Seattle Times

There can be no separate peace. " The late Tyree Scott

Larry and Tyree Scott at a Rainer Valley demonstration 1975. Photo courtesy CAMP

In response, Tyree and UCWA organized demonstrations at Seattle Central Community College that lasted about a week. Every day, the demonstrators showed up in the early morning at the work sites. Picket lines were established around the perimeter of the site. Demonstrators entered the work site and physically shut the sites down. Fights broke out between construction workers and demonstrators.

Larry Gossett was arrested three times that week. Roberto Maestas brought his students from the ESL Program to get a hands-on experience in civil disobedience. Roberto too was arrested, the handcuffs squeezed tightly on his wrists, making it very uncomfortable. Bob Santos was present in his official capacity as Vice Chair of the Seattle Human Rights Commission but was there only to observe.

At one of the demonstrations, Bob stood on the picket line. What had been planned as a non-violent demonstration turned ugly when white construction workers started throwing chunks of wood at the demonstrators below. The news media filmed the demonstrators climbing up the ladders onto the site at the college. Larry Gossett was filmed with a rebar in his hands. On one side, the construction workers in their hard hats, on the other side, demonstrators with makeshift weapons. A white construction worker challenged the charging demonstrators and was attacked. Bob stopped to look out for that construction worker until medical help arrived. The tactical response squad, complete with ominous dark shields, chased and hunted down the demonstrators.

When Bob climbed down the ladder, he noticed Tyree, Todd Hawkins, and Michael Ross handcuffed near a tree. Michael Ross told the police that Bob was with them. Bob insisted that he was only an observer, that he was the Vice Chair of the Seattle Human Rights Commission. It meant nothing to the police. And so, Bob was arrested, handcuffed, and hauled off to jail.

At the jail, the arresting officer told the group that they could leave once they signed citations for trespassing. Todd Hawkins told the cop that the group wouldn't sign the citations and were going to stay in jail. But not Bob. He grabbed the pen and signed the citation, telling Hawkins he had a wife and kids at home.

On July 13, 1972, after a week of demonstrations at Seattle Central Community College, Judge Lindberg took notice and ordered his Court Order Advisory Committee to include two representatives from UCWA. In addition, Judge Lindberg gave significant power to UCWA to oversee the implementation of union apprenticeship programs. It was a significant decision in labor history, which led to the desegregation of the area's building trades unions.

In December of 1974, Tyree Scott and the United Construction Workers Association took to the streets once again, this time to shut down a sewer project in Rainier Valley. For one week, the demonstrators showed up at the site, blocking the entrances, demanding that five minority heavy equipment operators be hired. The police were called each day. Negotiations went nowhere.

On February 12, 1975, UCWA showed up in the early morning and closed down the site. The demonstration ended when the police were called and arrests were made. Undeterred, UCWA showed up again on the morning of the next day, February 13, 1975 and again closed down the site. Once again, the police were called and arrests were made. In the two days of demonstrations, sixty-two demonstrators, including both Larry and Roberto, were arrested, each charged with disorderly conduct and trespassing.

Starting in the last week of March 1975, trials were held for the 62 demonstrators who had been arrested. They were tried in groups of two or three. Some had lawyers while others acted as their own attorneys. Over twenty trials were held.

During one trial, Roberto, who was sitting in the audience, refused to stand when the judge entered the courtroom. He was ordered to leave. He left quietly.

At Doug Chin's trial, Tyree announced to the crowd in the courtroom that the arrest and verdict were unjust, that they were leaving and taking Doug with them. The crowd did leave and Doug left with them. Doug was later found guilty and received a suspended sentence, contingent upon no arrests for the next year. He never served any time.

While the UCWA trials were going on, the 30-year-old Larry Gossett got married to 21-year-old Rhonda Oden.

The wedding invitation read, "To us the law of life is the struggle. This is why the love we have for one another is best expressed through our commitment to dedicate our lives to the struggle of oppressed and exploited peoples everywhere."

Father Michael Holland married Larry and Rhonda on March 25, 1975 in a traditional Catholic wedding held at the Immaculate Conception Church. Father Holland, known as the "activist priest," had been arrested before at a UCWA demonstration at the airport. Larry's best man was Roberto Maestas. When interviewed by the Seattle Times, Roberto gave glowing praise to Larry, stating, "He's the beloved son of the Black community; the Chicano community too. The saying in the Chicano community is that when you're in trouble and everything else fails, call Larry Gossett."

On April 9, 1975, Roberto went to trial. He was found guilty. His sentencing was deferred on the condition that he stay clean for one year. The next day, Larry went to trial. He served as his own attorney. He was found not guilty. It was those contradictory outcomes that eventually led to all of the convictions being thrown out.

Throughout his life, Tyree Scott played a major role in raising the political consciousness of the Gang of Four. His acts of civil disobedience served as an inspiration to both Roberto Maestas and Bernie Whitebear in their respective decisions to occupy the old Beacon Hill Elementary School and Fort Lawton. His persistence in fighting for equality in the construction trades inspired Larry Gossett and Bob Santos to join the cause.

Scott suffered for many years with prostate cancer but he continued his life-long activism until his death on June 19, 2003.

It was those contradictory outcomes that eventually led to all of the convictions being thrown out.

Larry and Rhonda 1975. Photo courtesy Gossett family

Chapter 20: United Farm Workers

In 1970, the United Farm Workers (UFW) contacted the St. Peter Claver Center for office space. While the UFW had been an organizing presence in the Yakima Valley since 1966, it had not been visible in the Seattle area. But with national boycotts of non-union grapes and lettuce, the UFW had sent people from Delano, California --Sara Welch, Nancy Welch, Fred Ross, and Dale Van Pelt, a Methodist minister--to Seattle to coordinate the boycotts.

Immediately, the UFW recruited Chicano student activists such as Roberto Maestas to the St. Peter Claver Center to connect campus activism to community activism. Meetings were held at the St. Peter Claver Center to organize the boycotts. Every Saturday, a group of picketers targeted local Safeways, urging shoppers to not buy non-union grapes and later, non-union lettuce.

It was fortuitous to the UFW to have their offices at the St. Peter Claver Center. The rights of farm workers was an issue that found support with Tyree Scott, Larry Gossett and the United Construction Workers Association. Larry took his turn on the picket line at the Safeway on Rainier and Genesee.

Bob Santos was well acquainted with the farm workers cause. Anita Santos, his wife at the time, was the niece of Philip Vera Cruz. Vera Cruz and Larry Itliong, both Filipino union organizers, had organized the first walk out of Filipino workers in California and had joined forces with the UFW. Itliong and Vera Cruz visited Seattle often to coordinate the lettuce boycott at Safeway stores and visited with Bob where they would talk for hours about the farm workers movement.

Bob, as the chair of city's Human Rights Commission, used his newly formed network of business people and members of the Human Rights Commission to arrange meetings with the UFW staff to promote the farm worker rights movement.

Bob, Roberto and Larry. Photo by Ruthann Kurose

Chapter 21: Fort Lawton

In 1964, Secretary of Defense Robert McNamara announced plans to surplus the army base at Fort Lawton. For more than eighty years, Fort Lawton had been used as a military base through World War I, World War II, and the Korean War. But the army base was no longer needed because military operations had been transferred from Fort Lawton to Fort Lewis.

The following year, Congressman Brock Adams introduced a bill to transfer the Fort Lawton property to the City of Seattle at no cost. The City of Seattle had envisioned using the military site as a city park. In 1968, however, the military announced plans to convert the property to an Anti-Ballistic missile base. A group of Magnolia residents, Citizens for a Fort Lawton Park, organized to fight the proposed missile base and to support the conversion of the site to a park. In December 1968, after Senator Henry Jackson intervened on the group's behalf, the military dropped its plans.

On November 20, 1969, approximately eighty Native Americans took control of Alcatraz Island in the San Francisco Bay Area. Thousands of supporters eventually joined the occupation. Approximately one month earlier, the San Francisco Indian Center burned down, leaving the Bay Area's urban Native Americans cut off from necessary social and educational programs. Attention focused on Alcatraz, the notorious federal prison, which had closed in 1963. The occupation would last for nearly eighteen months, from November 20, 1969 until June 11, 1971.

These Native Americans took Alcatraz, reclaimed it as Native American land, and called attention to the social problems that urban Native Americans faced. Demands were made to turn Alcatraz into a cultural park and Native American social and education center. The federal government turned it down as too unrealistic. So the occupation continued. Representing dozens of Native American nations around North America, the occupiers called themselves Indians of All Tribes.

The takeover at Alcatraz brought public attention to problems faced by urban Native Americans. Starting with the Eisenhower administration, government policies forced Native Americans away from tribal lands and into the cities, where the Bureau of Indian Affairs promised resettlement aid and job training. But urban Native Americans were given inadequate housing and limited help in transitioning from life on the reservation to life in the city. Native Americans, as a group, faced lower life expectancies than any other ethnic group.

The takeover at Alcatraz was an inspiration to Native American leaders in Seattle like Bob Satiacum and Bernie Whitebear. Like their counterparts in the Bay Area, Native Americans in Seattle lacked a Native American center, which they could take ownership of. Fort Lawton was their Alcatraz.

Bernie had resigned as Executive Director of the Seattle Indian Health Board early in 1970 to devote full time to obtaining land for a Native American community center. Meanwhile, Senator Henry Jackson was sponsoring a bill, which would transfer surplused military land at no cost to cities for parks and recreation. The City of Seattle wanted the land for a park because of its sweeping views of Elliot Bay and the Olympic Mountains.

In 1970, as Senator Jackson's bill was working its way through Congress, representatives of tribes and organizations in the Native American community from throughout western Washington met at St. Peter Claver Center. They formed a group, the United Indians People's Council, and strategized about getting access to Fort Lawton. Their claim to Fort Lawton was based on rights under 1865 U.S.-Indian treaties promising reversion of surplus military lands to their original owners. Native Americans, led by Bernie Whitebear, interpreted original owners to be themselves, the indigenous people of the region -- Native Americans of western Washington.

> *When the People's Council arrived at the entrance at Fort Lawton, the 392nd Military Police Company, dressed in full riot gear, which blocked their entry onto the Fort, met them.*

On March 8, 1970, the United Indians People's Council made their move. It was no secret that Bob Satiacum, Bernie Whitebear and about 100 Native Americans and supporters were going to Fort Lawton to make their claim. Given advance warning, the news media showed up. The Council enlisted the support of Jane Fonda, the actress, who had long been an Indian rights advocate. Fonda's presence brought 'star power' and only added to the curiosity of the news media as a story worth covering. When the People's Council arrived at the entrance at Fort Lawton, the 392nd Military Police Company, dressed in full riot gear, blocked their entry onto the Fort.

The People's Council set up an encampment near the entrance. But while attention focused on the main gate, dozens of supporters entered the Fort from all sides. Some climbed the bluffs on the western edge of the Fort. Others, like Bernie Whitebear, scaled the fences. A small group of approximately 30 Native Americans and their supporters set up camp inside the fences and erected a teepee.

Bob Satiacum read the proclamation of the United Indian People's Council laying claim to Fort Lawton . He announced that the Council planned to use Fort Lawton as a center for Native American studies, a Native American university, and a center for ecology, a school, and a restaurant.

The military police eventually arrested those who had set up the camp and chased down other protesters roaming about the grounds.

INDIANS 'BROKE CAMP' TODAY OUTSIDE FORT LAWTON

Front page of April 2, 1970 Seattle Times. Photo courtesy Seattle Times

Seventy-two protesters, including Bernie Whitebear and Jane Fonda, were escorted to the post stockade, questioned, identified, and issued "letters of expulsion."

Newspaper accounts of the incident, headlined by such titles as "Indians Attack Fort" brought the much-needed public attention that Bernie had sought from throughout the world, evoking images of the American Wild West. Back at the St. Peter Claver Center, Bernie enlisted the support of the other organizations that held meetings there.

The takeover earned the respect of those progressive organizations.

Larry Gossett read about the takeover and was impressed. He talked with the members of the BSU and the Black Panther Party. They decided they needed to express their solidarity with their Native American brothers and sisters.

Toward the end of May 1970, Larry and thirteen members of the Black Panthers showed their support by climbing the fences and "trespassing" on the military grounds. It was a sight of contrasts --the Panthers were dressed in black leather coats, starched shirts and slacks while their Native American counterparts had tennis shoes and moccasins.

It was there, on the grounds of Fort Lawton, that Larry formally introduced himself to Bernie Whitebear. Bernie welcomed Larry and the Panthers. Larry noticed that Native Americans had set up teepees to sleep in. It was the first time that he had seen teepees, outside of what he had seen on television. This was the first of several visits, which Larry and the Black Panthers made to Fort Lawton over a three-month period in support of the Native American occupation.

Bernie arrested by military police 1970. Photo courtesy Seattle Post Intellegencer

For Larry, the "seeds of unity" were planted. It was an awakening of sorts, working together with other communities of color on these important community struggles to build a racial political union.

The United Indian People's Council played a game of cat-and-mouse with the military police at Fort Lawton. They had kept a base camp, just outside the fence. At various times, the protesters jumped the fence and roamed about the base property. The military police chased them, apprehended them, and expelled them from the base. Then the protestors returned and again were chased, apprehended, and expelled from the base. This went on for four months. Federal and city officials realized that the United Indian People's Council was not going away.

The occupation ended peacefully in June of 1970 when government officials agreed to meet with the United Indian People's Council over their concerns.

In July of 1971, formal negotiations began with the United Indian People's Council, the City of Seattle, and Congressional representatives over the development of a Native American cultural center at Fort Lawton. Bernie had worked hard, behind the scenes, to gather community support. Over 40 non-Native American organizations signed letters of support for the United Indians Peoples Council. Bernie traveled to Washington DC and found congressional support from Congressman Brock Adams, and Senators Warren Magnuson and Henry Jackson.

These negotiations went on for five months until November of 1971 where it was agreed that the City of Seattle would get their park and the United Indian People's Council would get a ninety-nine year lease to build a cultural center.

The United Indian People's Council later changed its name to the United Indians of All Tribes Foundation when it organized as a formal entity.

Their Native American counterparts at Alcatraz didn't fare as well. At Alcatraz, negotiations broke down. The government cut off electrical power to the island. A fire, of mysterious origin, destroyed several buildings on the island. People left the island. On June 11, 1971, the government forcibly removed the remaining fifteen people from the island.

It was a sight of contrasts -- the Panthers were dressed in black leather coats, starched shirts and slacks while their Native American counterparts had tennis shoes and moccasins.

Marilyn Sieber and Bernie attend the NW Indian Education Conference. Photo courtesy UIATF

Chapter 22: Seeds of Unity Planted

In May 1970, anti-war demonstrations occurred on campuses throughout the country to protest the U.S. military invasion of Cambodia. On May 4, 1970, National Guardsmen killed four students at Kent State University during an anti-war protest. The shootings at Kent State served to intensify the anti-war movement. In Seattle, anti-war protests occurred throughout the week, shutting down the campus, spilling onto the interstate freeway, and sending thousands of protesters on the express lanes to downtown Seattle.

As President of the BSU, Larry Gossett had worked closely with Chip Marshall and Nick Licata of the Seattle Liberation Front on the UW campus. In March 1970, the BSU, with the support of the Seattle Liberation Front and other minority student organizations, shut down the campus over a wrestling match, which the UW had scheduled with Brigham Young University. The BSU was particularly upset with the religious practices of the Church of Latter Day Saints (Mormon), which prevented African Americans from becoming ministers in their churches. The wrestling match was cancelled.

When plans for a massive anti-war rally were developed, the Seattle Liberation Front reached out to the BSU and the Black Panther Party in a show of solidarity.

On May 8, 1970, over 15,000 protesters stopped traffic on Interstate 5, including 300 African American students mobilized by Larry Gossett and others connected with the BSU and the Black Panther Party. Larry was one of the featured speakers at the anti-war rally.

On May 15, 1970, the anti-war movement took on added significance for Larry when two African American students were killed at Jackson State University.

Bob Santos, in his role as the Vice Chair of the Seattle Human Rights Commission, came to the march as an official observer. As the demonstrators marched onto the freeway, Bob was in a city car with Phil Hayasaka and Father Harvey McIntyre, following a bus carrying the riot squad. Bob watched on a Capitol Hill overpass as the bus stopped. The riot squad spilled out onto the freeway below and began herding the demonstrators onto the express lanes. The march was peaceful.

Juggling his community involvement and his campus activism, Larry Gossett still found time to be a student. Larry graduated at the end of June 1971 with a Bachelor of Arts degree. He became the first UW student to obtain a degree in African American Studies. In fact, not only Larry, but also the other founders of the BSU had been successful as students. Of the thirteen founders of the BSU, eleven graduated.

Larry's involvement in campus politics had earned him the respect of minority administrators such as Dr. Samuel Kelly and Bill Hilliard at UW. In September 1970, before he had his B.A., he was hired to oversee the Black Student Division in the newly created Equal Opportunity Program (EOP) under the Office of Minority Affairs.

When Larry entered the UW in 1964, there were very few students of color. But by 1971, the University's EOP Program opened the doors for many students of color. In addition to the Black Student Division, there was the Chicano Student Division, Asian Student Division, and Native American Student Division.

Larry learned about the struggles of other minority students. One of the counselors in the Asian Student Division was Silme Domingo.

Larry and Silme developed a close friendship, finding common ground in their status as students of color in a mostly white educational institution and as political activists in their respective communities. Larry brought Silme to Frank's Landing to get familiar with the Indian Fishing Rights issue. He introduced Silme to Tyree Scott. Silme had become involved in organizing Alaska cannery workers.

Later, the Alaska Cannery Workers Association and the United Construction Workers Association, along with the United Farm Workers, would form the Northwest Labor and Employment Law Office (LELO).

In 1971, Roberto Maestas received his master's degree in Latin American Studies from the UW. In September 1971, other Latino activists, including Roberto Gallegos and Juan Bocanegra, looking for someone to direct a newly formed English-as-a-Second-Language (ESL) program at South Seattle Community College (SSCC), recruited Roberto.

By then, Roberto had developed a reputation as a political activist. Not content with just teaching English, Roberto infused his ESL classes with discussions about civil rights and the struggles of other communities of color. He brought in Al Bridges and Billy Frank to talk about fishing rights. He brought in Bob Santos to talk about the International District. He brought Tyree Scott to talk about worker's rights.

But when Tyree showed to speak in Roberto's class, Roberto found an unusual challenge. Tyree was from Texas and had a pronounced southern drawl, so pronounced that Roberto had to get a black person to interpret what Tyree was saying to him so he could then interpret what had been said in Spanish to the students.

By this time, Bob, Bernie, Larry, and Roberto had all found their way to the St. Peter Claver. Although the four had crossed paths at the St. Peter Claver Center, they barely knew each other. Larry and Roberto knew each other because of the sit-in at Franklin High School and they were both on the UW campus. Larry and Bernie had earned some notoriety for their roles in the occupations at Franklin High School and Fort Lawton. Bob was known by the others as the nice guy who opened the doors for us at the St. Peter Claver Center.

Roberto's first impressions of Bob were not positive. Bob was with the City Human Rights Commission when Roberto saw him for the first time. Roberto was skeptical of the Human Rights Commission and considered Bob to be a "lackey of the system."

But when Roberto saw Bob at the St. Peter Claver Center, he changed his mind about Bob, deciding that "he was on our side so he must be okay."

In 1973, Larry Gossett was still the lead supervisor for the Black Student Division at the UW but found that his time and interest were taking him away from his campus job. He used his vacation days to march in demonstrations and be involved in the community. His bosses at the UW, Bill Hilliard and Dr. Samuel Kelly, took Larry aside on numerous occasions, telling him to "cool it."

It was during this time that Larry Gossett and Roberto Maestas became close friends. Larry and Roberto had developed reputations as progressive leaders of their own ethnic communities. Roberto brought Larry to Frank's Landing to get him involved in the Native American Fishing Rights struggle. When Roberto decided to visit the leaders of the American Indian Movement at the Pine Ridge Reservation at Wounded Knee, he invited Larry to go with him. But Larry couldn't go because he still was the Director of the Black Student Division at the UW. He regretted not going and began to wonder if he was really being effective as a revolutionary by staying on campus.

> *Bernie noted that the gas shortage had little effect on poor people who couldn't afford to buy a car, let alone to buy a gallon of gas.*

Larry decided that as a revolutionary, he needed to be in the community. He believed that he couldn't do the progressive work in the community from the 'ivory tower.' As a college administrator, Larry was well paid. But his principles were more important. So, in the summer of 1973, Larry turned his back on his well-paying job and took on unemployment benefits.

In 1973, Larry, Roberto, and several like-minded Asian, Chicano, and African American activists such as Paul Patu, Sharon Maeda, Mayumi Tsutakawa, Ruben Soliz, and Juan Bocanegra, formed the first Third World Coalition. They began meeting regularly at El Centro de La Raza to study and discuss domestic and international issues that affected all peoples of color. Calling themselves a "people's revolutionary-oriented movement," the Third World Coalition supported grass roots people's liberation movements in Africa, Latin America, and Asia.

Larry, with his bushy Afro, and Roberto, with his bright red bandana, were very visible supporters of almost every demonstration

or protest in the early seventies. On October 11, 1973, both Roberto and Larry, representing the Third World Coalition, spoke at a pro-Palestinian rally at the UW in support of Palestinian self-determination.

Both Larry and Roberto counted themselves as supporters of the Native American movement. They had both reached out to Bernie Whitebear as members of the Third World Coalition to show their support.

On February 28, 1974, Bernie joined Larry and Roberto at a press conference held at El Centro to observe the first anniversary of the occupation of the city of Wounded Knee, South Dakota by members of the American Native American Movement. All

Bob, Harold Belmont, Roberto, and Bernie South African Consulate. Photo by Dean Wong

three criticized the press for ignoring Wounded Knee and for focusing exclusively on the effects that the then gas shortage had on the American middle class. Bernie noted that the gas shortage had little effect on poor people who couldn't afford to buy a car, let alone to buy a gallon of gas.

In 1977, Larry was instrumental in organizing MOVE (Making Our Votes Effective), the first local multi-ethnic, local electoral-based organization, to make a difference in that year's mayoral campaign. Those involved in MOVE decided that of the two candidates for mayor, Charles Royer and Paul Schell, Royer was more progressive and would be more accountable to communities of color. MOVE rallied their respective communities to vote for Charles.

MOVE had made a difference. Royer acknowledged the role played by MOVE. Several members of MOVE landed jobs in his first administration. This show of unity proved to Larry that coalition building between communities of color was essential to holding political power. MOVE continued to put pressure on Mayor Royer to make more money available to minority communities.

Each of them, Gang of Four, were charismatic and passionate leaders for change in their own communities. Together they were and continue to be the face of uniqueness of Seattle's progressive movement-a multiracial and powerful alliance of women and men of color, activists, workers and students.

Michael Woo
Founder, Got Green and Co-Founder, LELO (Legacy of Equality, Leadership and Organizing)

AGENCIES AT
GROUND ZERO
PART IV

Old Beacon Hill school now El Centro de la Raza

CHAPTER 23: El Centro de la Raza

In the summer of 1972, South Seattle Community College announced cutbacks in funding that led to the cancellation of its ESL Program. College administrators were not particularly pleased with the social justice component that Roberto had added to the ESL Program. Roberto wanted to continue the program but there was no place in the Latino community to house it. Roberto and other Latino activists, such as Roberto Gallegos and Juan Bocanegra, noted that while there were social services available to Latinos, such services were scattered throughout the city and did not address the particular social needs of Latinos.

One evening, Roberto went for a drink with Gallegos and Bocanegra at La Hacienda, a Mexican restaurant on Beacon Hill, a couple of blocks away from the old Beacon Hill Elementary School. When Roberto first came to Seattle in the early fifties, he played basketball on the outside courts of Beacon Hill Elementary School. The old Beacon Hill Elementary School had served thousands of children. When a new Beacon Hill Elementary School was built, the old school was abandoned.

Roberto believed that the school was a perfect place to establish a community center.

It was clear to Roberto and the other Latino activists that occupation was a viable option. Roberto had been present at Franklin High School when Larry Gossett and the BSU took over the Principal's office to demand educational equality for Franklin's African American students. He was on the UW campus when Larry and the BSU occupied the administration offices to demand educational equality for UW's African American students. When Native Americans occupied Alcatraz, Roberto took note. He especially paid attention when Bernie Whitebear and the United Indian People's Council occupied Fort Lawton.

On October 11, 1972, Roberto and 50 or so students and staff from the ESL program made their move. While October 11, 1972 was known in the United States as Columbus Day, October 11 was celebrated in Mexico as La Raza Day--El Dia A La Raza --the Day of the Races.

A phone call was directed to the Facilities Manager of the Seattle School District. He was told that there was a group interested in leasing or even buying the abandoned Beacon Hill school. The group wanted a tour of the building. The Facilities Manager came to the school at 8 am to show the building to the interested group. A custodian opened the doors of the old Beacon Hill School. Sensing something was up, the custodian gave the keys to the building to Roberto and told him to lock up when he was done.

Suddenly, a large group of fifty or so rushed into the building. Chicano students from the UW drove down to Beacon Hill. Responding to a phone message from Roberto, Larry Gossett came with twelve other African American activists including John Gillmore, Eddie Rye, Todd Hawkins, and Tyree Scott to offer their support. Bob Santos got a call from Roberto as well to get the support of the Human Rights Commission.

And last but not least, the media was called by Roberto and the takeover of the Beacon Hill school made the noon news.

Officials of the Seattle School District were not pleased. The occupiers took shifts, maintaining a constant presence at the old school. The building, vacant for several years, had no electricity and no running water. Rats ran rampant through the hallways. When Larry Gossett saw the rats, he was ready to leave. But he told himself that true revolutionaries had to endure these little hardships for the greater good and so he stayed.

The occupiers were very organized--while one group occupied the school, another group entered into formal negotiations with the City of Seattle and the Seattle School District. Bob Santos lobbied the Seattle Human Rights Commission to support negotiations between the City and Roberto's group. The group formally organized, filing articles of incorporation, to become a non-profit organization. The group called itself, "El Centro de la Raza," the Center for all Races.

One of those who signed the Articles of Incorporation was Larry Gossett, the only non-Chicano listed.

In November 1972, Estela Ortega was working in a real estate office in Houston, Texas. She received a note, written by Roberto Maestas that read, "Chicanos Occupy School. Come Visit." Estela had just met Roberto on Labor Day at a national conference,

"La Raza Uniada," in which Latino activists gathered to consider forming an alternative national political party. She decided to come to Seattle for a visit. Sparks flew and wasting no time, on December 10, 1972, Roberto and Estela were married at the old Beacon Hill School. Estela quit her job at the insurance company in Houston and moved to Seattle.

In early 1973, Roberto and the newly formed El Centro de la Raza were beginning to get frustrated at the slow pace of negotiations with the City. An initial vote by the Seattle City Council rejected a proposal to lease the building to El Centro. Roberto and other Chicano activists showed up at City Council meetings, at one point, even occupying the City Council chambers, in an effort to pressure City officials into turning the property over to them. The Seattle City Council finally agreed to lease the building to El Centro but the Mayor refused to sign the lease.

On February 6, 1973, Roberto, Larry, and 50 other El Centro supporters staged a five-hour occupation of Mayor Wes Uhlman's City Hall reception area. Mayor Uhlman had written the City Council a letter, stating that he would not sign a lease until he was assured that there was proper funding to operate the center. The City Council had previously approved $87,000 in Model Cities funding to pay for the rehabilitation of the building. The Urban League had promised to pay $4,000. But it was still $40,000 short of the funding necessary.

Uhlman refused to meet so the group of approximately 50 decided to stay. Finally, the mayor said that he would meet with five of the group and did so for 40 minutes. After the meeting, the group returned to the reception area. Roberto said that he and the others were too tired to leave. The police were called and 18 people including Roberto, Estela Ortega, Larry Gossett, Raul Anaya, Gloria Rivera, Juan Bocanegra, and Roberto Gallegos were arrested and cited for criminal trespass.

Eventually, after months of negotiations and outside pressure, a deal was struck. The school district agreed to lease the surplused school building to the City of Seattle for $1; the City of Seattle agreed to then lease the surplused school building to Roberto and his group for $1.

Thus, El Centro de la Raza was born.

In 1973, the group that took over the old Beacon Hill School had a lot of work to do. Conditions at the old school, built in 1914, were far below building code standards. Volunteers took turns, maintaining a 24-hour fire watch. El Centro applied for and received a Model Cities grant to make improvements in bringing the building up to code. Childcare services were started off site. The ESL program was restarted. A food bank was started. Volunteers started an information and referral service. For the first few years, volunteers provided all services.

After El Centro's first Executive Director quit, Roberto stepped in and took over as Executive Director, a position he would hold for more than thirty-five years. After two years operating as an all-volunteer organization, El Centro obtained a $12,500 operating grant in 1974 from the Community Services Administration to provide services to the community. Under Roberto's leadership, the agency grew to a multi-million dollar agency serving what he always termed "the beloved community."

Bob, Ricardo Sanchez, Henry Cisneros, and Roberto. Photo courtesy El Centro de la Raza

CHAPTER 24: International District Improvement Association

The International District (Chinatown) had long been the first home for the area's Pan-Asian community, a place where the first generation of Japanese, Chinese, and Filipino immigrants settled in America and raised their families. By 1971, what had once been a thriving neighborhood was in a state of urban decay. Closer to the commercial core, hotels were closed and abandoned, some torn down for parking lots, leaving gaps in the continuous built-up street walls. The construction of Interstate 5 in the 1960's physically divided the area and eliminated businesses, homes, and churches. Families left Chinatown, moving into Beacon Hill and Rainier Valley.

In 1968, the International District Improvement Association or "Inter*Im" had been formed by a group of business people, including Ben Woo, Tomio Moriguchi, and Don Chin, to revitalize and promote the commercial potential of the International District. Inter*Im received a small Model Cities Program grant and had opened up an office in a storefront in the N.P. Hotel, staffed by a part-time Model Cities program coordinator.

In 1970, Inter*Im applied for full funding from Model Cities to hire a full-time director, support staff, and operating capital. Coincidentally, Bob had just been elected as a voting member of the Model Cities Board of Directors. When the Model Cities Board met to vote on the proposal, there was a 14 to 14 tie. Board Chair Judge Charles V. Johnson, an African American, broke the tie and voted against the motion to fund Inter*Im. This decision angered the International District representatives who attended the meeting. They felt the decision was a vote against the Asian American community. Asian community members applied intense lobbying efforts with the City of Seattle, which administered the Model Cities Program.

A second Inter*Im proposal was submitted to the Model Cities Board in 1971 and was approved for full funding.

When Bob was approached to become its Executive Director, Inter*Im had been in a state of flux with staff turnovers, going through two coordinators and two directors in three years. In October of 1971, Bob Santos was recruited by Shigeko Uno and Jacquie Kay to become the Executive Director of Inter*Im.

Several business people on the Inter*Im board questioned Bob's experience and ability to work in promoting the commercial interests of the International District. But what Bob did bring to the table was his record of advocacy, his ability to articulate on behalf of equal rights and equal opportunities. Inter*Im needed a leader who could advocate on the behalf of the International District.

About a month after Bob was hired to be Inter*Im's Executive Director, King County officials announced that a multi-purpose domed sports stadium would be built at a site on King Street in the neighborhood.

Bob and wife Sharon Tomiko enjoy the festivities at the Bon Odori Japanese festival. Photo by Johnny Valdez

Suddenly, Bob's job became that much harder.

Like their Latino and African American counterparts, young Asian Americans had become heavily involved in campus activism. In the spring of 1969, the Asian Coalition for Equality challenged admission policies at the UW, which denied minority status to Asian Americans.

In 1970, Asian American students, led by Alan Sugiyama and Mike Tagawa at Seattle Central Community College (SCCC), organized the Oriental Student Union and demanded more Asian American faculty and an Asian American history class. A six-hour takeover of the administration building by the Oriental Student Union led to the arrest of five Asian American demonstrators.

These young Asian activists decided that it was necessary to connect back to the community outside the college campus. Young college-aged activists took up revitalization of the International District as a cause. After King County decided to build a domed sports stadium at the edge of the International District, there were increasing concerns about the potential negative impacts which the stadium would create--increased traffic, rising property values, gentrification, crime.

Sabino Cabildo began holding meetings at the Filipino Drop-In Center to organize Filipino residents to protest their potential displacement by the development of the stadium. Peter Bacho, then a law student, filed a class action lawsuit on behalf of International District residents, citing the County's failure to consider the environmental impacts, in an attempt to stop construction of the stadium. But in September 1972, the lawsuit was dismissed. The construction of the domed stadium was now a foregone conclusion but these activists were not going away quietly.

On November 2, 1972, the groundbreaking ceremony for the domed stadium, named the "Kingdome," drew almost every major officeholder in the state. While the area's public officials such as King

The march to H.U.D. by over 150 protesters including Angel Doniego, Sherrie Chinn, Allison Alfonzo, Reme Bacho, Norris Bacho, Bob, and Al Sugiyama. Photo by Eugene Tagawa, Asian Family Affair

County Executive John Spellman and Seattle City Council President Liem Tuai congratulated themselves and posed for pictures, a group of 25 to 35 Asian American demonstrators, including the Sugiyama brothers, Bacho brothers, Domingo brothers, Sharon Maeda, Mayumi Tsutakawa, and Ruthann Kurose, stood on the sidelines, heckling and chanting, to disrupt the proceedings. Mud balls were thrown at the politicians. One demonstrator, Nemesio Domingo, was arrested for swearing and giving "the finger" to a policeman. Charges were later dropped.

None of the Asian activists really thought they could stop the Kingdome from being built. But they did want to draw attention to the problems faced by the International District--lack of decent housing, no social services, and an urban neighborhood in a state of decline. After the demonstration, a meeting was held later that evening by the activists at the St. Peter Claver Center to plan the next move. Some suggested another demonstration at the Kingdome site but others felt that media attention had peaked at the groundbreaking ceremony.

Instead, the group, calling themselves, Concerned Asians for the International District, decided to take the offensive and make demands for decent elderly, low-income housing. They decided to use the construction of the Kingdome as a way to get the attention of government officials to fund programs and services to preserve the International District.

It was Bob who suggested a visit by residents and supporters to the local HUD (U.S. Department of Housing and Urban Development) office. Bob set up an appointment with HUD officials, who agreed to meet with a small International District delegation.

Twelve days later, on November 14, 1972, a rally was held at the site of what would later be Hing Hay Park. The group had decided to hold a rally to mobilize supporters, many of whom were Asian American college students, and march to the HUD offices. More than 150 demonstrators gathered for the march. Larry Gossett came to show his support at the invitation of Silme Domingo. Roberto Maestas showed up as well, taking time off from the occupation at the old Beacon Hill School.

The march started from the International District and then proceeded north on Second Avenue. Protesters held signs that read, "Save the I.D," "Doom the Dome," and "A Parking Lot is Not a Home."

An Associated Press photographer took a picture of one sign that read, "HUM BOWS NOT HOT DOGS!" When Larry Gossett saw the sign, he went up to the elderly Filipino resident carrying the cardboard placard and asked, "Hum bows, what's that?"

Somebody shouted, "Asian soul food." Larry smiled and said, "I can dig it."

When the march reached HUD offices at the Arcade Plaza, the original plan called for Bob and the small International District delegation to meet with HUD officials while the marchers waited downstairs. But the marchers would have none of that. All 150 or so marchers took the elevators to the fourth floor. They crowded into the HUD conference room. It was standing room only while those who couldn't make it into the conference room, filled the corridor, straining to hear what was said.

Marshall Majors, HUD Administrator, met with the group. While the group demanded immediate action to rehabilitate buildings like the Atlas, Panama, Eastern, and N.P. hotels, HUD officials told the crowd that the City had to prioritize the International District as a neighborhood in need of low-income elderly housing. It wasn't what the crowd wanted to hear. But it did give the group some direction and did open the dialogue for the International District activists to find federal dollars for low-income housing.

Bob hired some of the young activists such as Elaine Ko and Shari Woo to organize the mainly elderly Filipino and Chinese residents living in the hotels and apartments, badly in need of repair or renovation. These organizing efforts resulted in the creation of the International District Housing Alliance.

In early 1973, Bob met with government officials on a variety of issues, primarily in finding ways to mitigate the impacts of the Kingdome on the International District. Bob became a regular speaker at City Council and County Council hearings, testifying in support of low-income housing. Lobbying efforts by Bob and other community leaders with the County resulted in funding for a community clinic, the International District Health Clinic. Working with social workers and students from the U of W, Bob invited the first director of the newly formed Asian Counseling and Referral Service to share space at the Inter*Im office.

In the summer of 1975, Bob decided to build a community garden. The residents of the International District needed a place to grow their vegetables. There was a barren hillside, rife with weeds and sticker bushes. Bob managed to talk Danny Woo, the owner of the land, into leasing the property to Inter*Im for $1. Now that he had the land for a garden, the next step was to construct it. He approached the railroad companies for railroad ties to shore up the foundation. He approached the Longacres Race Track for manure to fertilize the soil.

Once Inter*Im got the materials, Bob put out the call for volunteers. It was volunteers who built the garden and the terraces. Residents, college students, employees from other social service agencies answered the call. Bob called Bernie Whitebear who brought the United Indians for All Tribes Foundation staff and the news media. The news headlines read, "Indians Build Garden for Asian Community." Bob called Roberto Maestas who sent some of the El Centro staff to help out.

Inter*Im, under Bob's leadership, initiated important programs that have since continued to flourish – including building several hundred units of decent affordable housing for seniors and low income families in the neighborhood and throughout King County, working with health professionals to establish the International District Community Health Center; opening the Denise Louie Child Care Center; establishing several congregate meal programs for low income seniors; building the Danny Woo Community Garden and preserving the International District/Chinatown neighborhood for the pioneers who built it and for the generations to follow.

Bob continued as Executive Director until 1985 and returned to the agency again serving as Executive Director from 2000-2006 until his retirement.

> Working with 'Uncle Bob' for so many years, he never lost his fire -- a beloved icon in our community that will live on for many generations to come.

Elaine Ikoma Ko
former Executive Director of
Inter*Im Community
Development Association

CHAPTER 25: United Indians of All Tribes Foundation

The United Indians of All Tribes Foundation (UIATF) was founded in 1970 by a small group of Northwest Native Americans and their supporters, who engaged in the occupation of Fort Lawton. As noted earlier, their goal was to reclaim a land base for urban Native Americans living in and around Seattle. At the time, the old army base had been surplused by the federal government. When the property was surplused, the Army made it known that the "original" owners of the land should have the first rights to it.

In 1971, after gaining the support of U.S. Senators Warren Magnuson and Henry Jackson, a deal was struck which gave UIATF 20 acres of land, under a 99-year lease.

By 1973, the United Indians' People Council had become the UIATF, in part to honor the Alcatraz occupiers and Bernie was installed as its Executive Director. In early 1973, Bernie Whitebear began working with architects in developing a master plan for a Native American cultural community center.

Bernie, a member of the Colville Confederated Tribe, and Bob Satiacum, a member of the Puyallup Tribe, gathered tribal leaders and members across the Pacific Northwest to discuss the land known as Fort Lawton.

Despite traditional tribal differences, they were united in agreement that Native Americans were the "original" owners of the land under the authority of Indian treaties and other documents that were generated when the U.S. Army first built Fort Lawton.

While Bernie had succeeded in finding a place for a Native American community cultural center, that was only half the battle. He had to find the funding to make his vision a reality. He undertook a major fund-raising effort. Bernie negotiated with Governor Daniel J. Evans for a $1 million state construction grant. He applied for and received an $80,000 grant from the Seattle Arts Commission to install Native American artwork for the building's interior. He found funding from the City of Seattle, the Economic Development Administration, U.S. Department of Commerce, private donations from the Colville, Quinault, and Makah Tribes, and from corporations.

After the land was secured, the next major accomplishment for UIATF involved the construction of the Daybreak Star Indian Cultural Center.

As Bernie worked to find funding, his brother Lawney Reyes, worked with Northwest architects Arai Jackson to design the center. They developed a Master plan which was approved by the City, providing for the development of several facilities--the Daybreak Star Arts Center, the Heritage Resource Center which included an archives and library, a performing arts center, a restaurant, and the People's Lodge, a multi-use facility.

Daybreak Star Cultural Center photo by Joe Mabel

Ground breaking for the Daybreak Star Center took place on September 27, 1975 and was completed and dedicated on May 13, 1977.

The Center, nestled on the bluff overlooking Puget Sound, is one of the most majestic sites in the Northwest.

Daybreak Star Cultural Center houses the Great Hall, United Indians administrative offices, kitchen, the Art Mart and a permanent art collection depicting and featuring murals of Native Americans from the Southwest Nations, Southeast Nations, Northeast Nations, Plaines and Northwest Nations.

Through the years, UIATF developed a wide range of social services designed to meet the needs of Seattle's urban Native Americans including Head Start, Early Head Start, foster care, cultural and clinical therapy, substance abuse prevention and outpatient treatment, elderly and youth services.

Bernie continued as Executive Director until his death in 2002.

CHAPTER 26: Central Area Motivation Program

The Central Area Motivation Program (CAMP) grew out of the Civil Rights movement. Part of the new Civil Rights legislation was a mandate to provide funding support for federal anti-poverty agencies. The lead federal anti-poverty agency was named the Office of Economic Opportunity (OEO) and served to direct the federal government's national War on Poverty.

Many Central Area groups were prepared to take up such a challenge of working together to set up a program to fight poverty in Seattle's inner-city community. Activists and groups like Carole Richmond of Madrona Community Council, Ed Banks of Manor Minor Neighborhood Association, Reverend Samuel B. McKinney of Mt. Zion Baptist Church, Ed Pratt, CEO of the Seattle Urban League, and many more participated in the first meeting.

The leaders were multiracial, dynamic, and full of ideas on how to uplift the poor through housing, education, transit, and youth development programs.

The CAMP Community Coalition ended up being highly successful. In October 1964, CAMP became the first community action agency funded west of the Mississippi River. The community organizations and the thousands of people who supported the establishment of a new anti-poverty program rallied their support. The doors of CAMP opened on January 1965 to serve the people.

However, by the summer of 1978, CAMP, the area's primary anti-poverty African American social service agency, was in crisis mode. CAMP faced federal audits, possible criminal prosecutions, and loss of funds because of alleged mismanagement. The federal government took control over the agency. At the beginning of 1979, CAMP reemerged with proposals to streamline the agency to become financially transparent.

Central Area Motivational Program (CAMP). Photo by Joe Mabel

A new Executive Director was nominated to take control of CAMP. That new Executive Director was Larry Gossett, selected by the CAMP board on April 1, 1979.

Larry was very happy about this latest appointment. It represented the second time in his young life that he was able to leave employment in a large institution (City of Seattle) and return to the community to work with low-income Black families. Earlier (1973), he had resigned from the UW as an Administrator to be closer to the community.

He thought that as the Executive Director of CAMP, he could really get a strong poor people's movement going, his deep desire since leaving VISTA. He was fired up and ready to go!

By the time Larry took over CAMP in 1979, it had a great reputation for working hard to uplift inner-city minorities. Larry was successful at securing other funds like getting the Washington State government to fund its Low-Income Home Energy Assistance program (LIHEAP) to provide home heating assistance to low-income central and southeast Seattle residents. He also set up an employment training program, which helped nearly 300 people a month to return to school. He found money to expand CAMP's extremely popular youth advocacy program.

By the end of June 1979, CAMP was serving 700 families a month. Larry did clean up the mess he inherited and, under his leadership, restored the credibility of CAMP.

When Larry Gossett took over CAMP, its budget was $230,000 annually. When he left the agency 14 years later, its annual budget was $3.8 million. Over the years, Larry were able to enhance existing programs and to establish new programs to help serve the basic needs of the poor like the food bank, weatherization, youth, and employment programs.

Larry continued to serve as Executive Director from 1979 to 1993, resigning after he was elected to the King County Council.

THE GANG OF FOUR COMES OF AGE
PART V

The Power of Unity

The Four Amigos

Bernie Whitebear   Larry Gossett   Roberto Maestas   Bob Santos

Original Art By Al Doggett   Commissioned By Fremont Public Association

Courtesy Al Doggett, artist

CHAPTER 27: Comrades and Camaraderie

The 1980s ushered in the presidency of Ronald Reagan. President Reagan's economic policies, often referred to as "Reaganomics," made it tough for the survival of social service agencies. With increasing numbers of immigrants and refugees, the need for social services grew. The Reagan Administration cut taxes for the rich and slashed federal support to cities, cut the budget for low income housing in half, and eliminated the antipoverty Community Block Grant program, which had been the main source of funding for agencies like CAMP, Inter*Im, El Centro, and the United Indians of All Tribes Foundation.

By the early 1980s, the Gang of Four was firmly established in leadership roles in their respective communities.

Bob Santos was Executive Director of Inter*Im, Roberto Maestas was Executive Director of El Centro de la Raza, Bernie Whitebear, was Chief Executive Officer of the United Indians of All Tribes Foundation, and Larry Gossett was Executive Director of CAMP.

All four men had risen to the leadership of the foremost community-based agencies in their communities and were each seen as perhaps, the leading voice and advocate in their respective communities for the poor. Each of the four organizations had started out as grass-roots community groups and each had developed into multi-service agencies, fueled by an infusion of local, state, and federal funding from antipoverty revenue sources that were filtering resources to the communities.

And all four agencies were absolutely committed to grass-roots community organizing and agitation.

Public funds from national programs became available for state, county and city distribution. Funds from Government programs like Community Services Administration (CSA) and Housing and Urban Development (HUD) were allocated to the local governments. Program funds were then allocated to local non-profits after a series of hearings before the legislative bodies of cities, counties and state.

Larry, Bernie, Roberto and Bob attended countless hearings to testify on behalf of their anti-poverty programs. Their paths crossed often, particularly when appearing before the City Council finance committee hearings, testifying in support of funding for their respective agencies. City Council hearings were long, drawn out, repetitious events that were a "must attend" by the agencies requesting funds.

It soon became a 'contest' of which agency could influence the legislative body the most.

Roberto testified in Spanish. Bernie brought drummers who performed in the lobby of the City Council and could be heard loud and clear in the chambers. Larry brought supporters from CAMP wearing silk-screened T-shirts with CAMP's logo. Bob brought the Asian elderly who testified in dialect, translated in embellished form by Maxine Chan.

> *All four men had risen to the leadership of the foremost community-based agencies in their communities and were each seen as perhaps, the leading voice and advocate in their respective communities for the poor.*

With a funding environment that encouraged competition between minority communities for scarce government funding, the four minority Executive Directors, building on their past relationships and shared experiences as community activists, supported funding for all of their agencies, refused to be caught up in pitting one community against another. They agreed that whenever there was a public hearing, all four would show up, as a unified group.

They had a lot in common. As activists, they supported social causes that affected all low-income and minority people.

As directors of social service agencies, they knew that they had to find a more effective way of influencing government decisions. The tactics of political persuasion enhanced the tactics of political confrontation. They all had been rabble-rousers, political activists, and leaders who had relied on the tactics of political confrontation but had matured in their approach to social change.

Early in the seventies, Bernie contacted Bob to learn more about his Filipino heritage. Bob introduced Bernie to the lounge scene in the International District and as the two moved from the Gim Ling Restaurant to Four Seas, Quong Tuck, Silver Dragon, and Linyen lounges, Bernie mentioned to Bob: "Filipinos like to do the same thing as Indians: party."

Bob, Larry, Bernie, and Roberto democratic panel Seattle 1984. Photo courtesy El Centro de la Raza

Larry and Roberto had developed a close personal relationship through the years of struggle on the picket line. Each served as the best man for the other during their wedding ceremonies. While both men had amicable relationships with Bob and Bernie, it wasn't until the early 1980s when each had risen to directors of their community's leading social service agency, that they all became close friends. Their show of unity inspired other leaders in Seattle's communities of color.

The four began meeting on a regular basis, strategizing on ways to increase the resources available for their respective agencies and their constituents. They formed a coalition and began negotiating with local government, foundations, corporate-giving offices, and businesses to set aside a pot of money to be matched dollar for dollar by the Local Initiatives Support Group (LISC), an affiliate organization of the Ford Foundation, based in New York City. Bob had cultivated a relationship with LISC staff, which funded projects that encouraged collaborations between community development organizations and the private sector.

It became apparent that the four Executive Directors formed a unique and powerful coalition that had never happened anywhere else in the country. They met not only for coalition building but socially because they found that they had much in common and really liked being with and working with each other.

There was no one leader among the four. When an idea was mentioned by one of the four about an issue or event that needed the attention of the other three, there was discussion and, in most cases, likely consensus that the issue discussed would be accepted by the group.

Each of the four were often invited to speak at rallies, demonstrations, dinners, banquets, receptions, and community events and often times, on the program together. They all had that unique ability to inspire the crowds.

You are the heart and soul of our community.

Norm Rice
Former Mayor of Seattle

CHAPTER 28: Unity...in Comedy

In the fall of 1982, the Northwest Asian American Theatre (NWAAT), an Asian American performing arts organization, announced that it was producing a Holiday Community Showoff and invited performers and would-be performers with an opportunity to perform on stage.

When Bob read about the Community Showoff, he called Bernie, Larry, and Roberto and asked them if they wanted to do "something goofy."

The four began meeting at Quong Tuck Restaurant and began discussing what they would do for the Showoff. The first time around, they decided to put on a skit. They played Seattle City Council members at a committee hearing. They set their schedules, slotting rehearsal time a couple of months in advance. Each man showed up at every rehearsal, memorized their lines, and practiced, practiced, practiced, to get their timing down.

On the night of the Showoff, the audience at the Nippon Kan Theater was packed with friends and family of the performers, supporters of NWAAT, and other Asian community members. The Gang of Four, slated to perform last, waited patiently off stage as a parade of good singers and bad singers, and good dancers and bad dancers made their way on stage. Comedian Arnold Mukai served as the emcee. City Councilwoman Dolores Sibonga led a Christmas carol sing-along.

Finally, the Gang of Four was announced. Bernie was dressed as Councilwoman Jeanette Williams, complete with a dress, a shawl, a wig, and glasses. Roberto played the role of Councilman Sam Smith in a loud, bellowing voice without a hint of an accent. Larry played the role of Councilman George Benson, entering the stage with a guitar in his hand. The joke here was that the white Councilman Benson had the same name as the famous Black jazz guitarist. The audience roared with laughter at the sight of these four serious community leaders "acting goofy."

They were the hit of the Showoff. In reality, they were all frustrated actors. Each man was no stranger to being the center of public attention and comfortable in the spotlight. Now, bitten by the performing bug, the Gang of Four looked forward each year to come up with something novel to bring before audiences at NWAAT's Community Showoff.

"I Heard It From The Grapevine" performance by Larry, Bob, Roberto, Bernie, and Annie Galarosa NWAAT 1983. Photo courtesy Vera Ing

The next year, 1983, the Gang of Four rehearsed diligently for two months, lip-synching and dancing as the Pips to Annie Galarosa's Gladys Knight in "I Heard It Through the Grapevine." Despite practicing the routine over and over and over again, when it came to the actual performance, the guys were a little out of step. When the guys pulled the "Soul Train," the audience roared.

During the next ten years, the Gang of Four made it to every Community Showoff. Skits were performed with one-liners, corny puns, and political insider jokes. Sometimes, other minority community leaders such as Theresa Fujiwara, Emma Catague, Estela Ortega, and Kikora Dorsey would join them on stage.

One year, the Gang of Four debated the merits of white rice versus brown rice, which culminated with a cameo appearance by Seattle's African American Mayor, Norm Rice. Over the years, they performed with sombreros as the 'Four Amigos,' played as kids at a day care center, and as contestants in "The Dating Game," with Bob dressed in a fright wig as the prize.

The Gang of Four had public personas of hardcore radical activists who had physically taken over universities, schools, airports, and federal installations in support of their social causes. Their appearances at NWAAT's Community Showoff showed a different side of their character--their sense of humor. The audience had a lot of fun but not as much as the Gang of Four. The long hours of rehearsing cemented their everlasting bonds of friendship.

> *Their appearances at NWAAT's Community Showoff showed a different side of their character--their sense of humor.*

As their reputations as a group grew within the progressive community, names for them as a group surfaced. Joe Garcia, the Deputy Director of El Centro in the early eighties, started calling the four Directors, "the Gang of Four."

Ike Ikeda, long time Executive Director of the Atlantic Street Center referred to the four Executive Directors as the "Gang of Four" in an article he wrote for a local newspaper. Folks at El Centro started to refer to the four as the "Four Amigos." The names stuck.

> Yo Four Amigos, one of my favorite things about you all is that you support the women of our communities.
>
> "
>
> Ticiang Diangson
> feminist activist leader

Larry, Bob, and Bernie during skit at The Theater Off Jackson 1987. Photo courtesy NWAAT

CHAPTER 29: Gang of Four Inspires Others

Roberto and Bernie in Japan.
Photo courtesy Theresa Fujiwara

Inspired by the ability of the Gang of Four to work together across ethnic lines, other Executive Directors of non-profit organizations in the minority communities began meeting to find common ground. The numbers of organizations that started to meet on a regular basis reached twenty in number and began steadily increasing. The group incorporated as a non-profit organization in the early eighties under the title, "Minority Executive Directors Coalition of King County (MEDC)." In the first decade of its existence, MEDC relied on volunteers. Office space was provided by El Centro.

MEDC took on issues not only on a local scale but also on a broader, international scale. They took a stand on human rights issues such as supporting the anti-apartheid movement in South Africa.

Starting in the fall of 1984, MEDC sent representatives to weekly Sunday protests, coordinated by the Seattle Coalition Against Apartheid, outside the local South African consulate.

On Sunday, February 4, 1985, ten members of MEDC, including Larry, Bob, Bernie, and Roberto, were arrested and cited for criminal trespass at the South African Honorary Consulate.

In April of 1990, Richard Mar, an activist from the International District, was hired through a City of Seattle block grant to coordinate the activities and direction of MEDC. The motto became to "maintain unity in the community." With a staff person on board, MEDC acquired the necessary organizational capacity to conduct outreach, expand membership, establish committees, identify priorities, and coordinate activities as a viable advocacy agency.

In 1996, MEDC received its non-profit designation by the State of Washington. Dorry Elias was hired as its first Executive Director. With Dorry at its helm, MEDC eventually grew its membership to over 100 executive directors and administrators representing almost every major social service and advocacy organizations serving communities of color in King County.

MEDC became an influential advocacy entity for the coalition and its members. MEDC members and staff provided testimony before many city, county and state legislative bodies during the eighties and nineties. MEDC staff met with individual leaders from the private and public sectors throughout the state. It became the conscience on behalf of the communities of color to make the public and private sectors toe the line.

The four were not only activists on the local scene but were actively involved in national and or international issues as well. Silme Domingo and Gene Viernes were two young Filipino American activists who were working to expose human rights abuses of Filipino workers in the Philippines by the Ferdinand Marcos regime. They organized community members like Bob to stage frequent protests at the Philippine Embassy to oppose martial law, which Marcos had imposed on his country.

On June 1, 1981, Silme and Gene were murdered at their Seattle cannery workers union office. There were strong suspicions in the community that the Marcos regime had a role in their murders. Bob joined the Committee for Justice for Domingo Viernes, a group formed to tie President Marcos to what was believed to be assassinations of these activists.

After a decade of investigating the trail of funds that paid the murder for hire of Silme Domingo and Gene Viernes, Marcos, the former president of the Philippines, and his wife Imelda, were found complicit in U.S. District Court, for their roles in the assassination of the two Filipino American activists.

In the late 1980s-through the early 1990s, Roberto brought 41 delegations of Americans to Nicaragua to witness living conditions, visit hospitals and schools, and educate them about what was actually happening in that country. Roberto was concerned by the propaganda spewed by those advocating for the invasion of by the U.S. military into that Central American country. He felt that it was important to show that the people of Nicaragua supported the revolutionary government. Roberto may very well have prevented an invasion by US military forces in Nicaragua.

In 1992, the Gang of Four, along with Cheryl Ellsworth, a feminist, was invited by the Japanese Ministry of Foreign Affairs to provide Japanese government and business leaders with insights about grass-roots democracy, the relationships of American minority communities working with each other, and U.S.-Japan relations. Funded by the Japan Foundation Center for Global Partnership and the Sedaka Foundation of Seattle, the Mutual Exchange and Education Tour was designed to promote better understanding between Japan's and America's grassroots communities.

The tour came about for several reasons. During this period of time, Japan was experiencing an immigration surge that brought scores of workers from several countries, including the Philippines, South Korea, India and Middle East, in such numbers large enough to form their own minority communities. In addition, the early 1990s was a period of strained relations between Japan and the United States. Japan bashing first appeared in the 1960s, when Sony bought Columbia Pictures, and in the 1990s when Americans were buying more Toyotas, Hondas, and Sony TVs than ever before.

A local Japanese newspaper cover the delegation

The group from Seattle met with government and private officials, the press, and youth groups in a variety of formal and informal gatherings in a six-day period in Tokyo, Kyoto, and Kobe. The Gang of Four made written and oral presentations about their respective communities, their grass roots organizing, their ability to work together as a coalition, and their struggles as minorities to be accepted in a dominant white country. Of particular interest was the manner in which the ethnic leaders were able to organize their respective communities to fight for equal rights in the fields of education, employment and housing and how women were able to compete with their male counterparts.

Bernie talked about the sovereignty of the Indian Nation and the fact that Native American tribes had ownership of 56 million acres of prime mineral and vacation territory. Larry talked about the purchasing power of African Americas, as a whole, over $300 billion in 1991, and the contributions which African Americans made to science and industry. Bob shared his experiences working in the International District of Seattle where Chinese, Japanese, Filipino, Korean and Vietnamese of the first, second and third generations needed to work together for the preservation of their separate cultures and the survival of their historic community. Roberto explained the problems Nintendo owner Hiroshi Yamauchi was having purchasing the majority share of the Seattle Mariners Major League Baseball team while there were community concerns about Nintendo's hiring practices. Cheryl Ellsworth provided insights about the women's movement in Seattle.

Gang of Four delegation to Japan 1992. Photo courtesy Theresa Fujiwara

The Gang of Four, by spending ten days together, really bonded. They were assigned a van, translators, and representatives from the Japanese Foundation Center for Global Partnership, and at times the local media. The delegation spent evenings at Tokyo nightclubs and the finest restaurants. At an exclusive nightclub in Tokyo, Bob fulfilled a life's dream when he was invited up to the stage to sing with a local jazz band.

There were cherished moments, one being when Larry translated every comment and explanation given by the translator who spoke perfect English, in English. Roberto had dozens of questions for everyone they met. Bernie and Roberto, as recommended by Bob, ordered massages in their rooms. When the masseuse knocked on their doors they heard, in a loud voice in English, "Ready for massage, no sex."

During a dinner in Kobe at an exclusive restaurant on the top floor of a four-star hotel, Roberto kept sending the waiter back to the kitchen for more wasabi, the ultra-hot Japanese mustard. After five trips to the kitchen, the chef finally came out with a large bowl of wasabi. To his amazement, the chef watched Roberto dump the whole bowl of wasabi on his rice like gravy. Others in the dining room crowded around the table to watch Roberto, sans chopsticks, devour the rice and wasabi with his fingers.

When the Gang of Four returned home from the tour, they decided to meet for lunch or dinner every month to stay connected. When they did meet, they would each talk for five minutes about the issues they were working on at their agencies and then spend rest of the time teasing each other about nothing of importance.

There were a few nights of karaoke at the Bush Garden where Bernie did 'Elvis;' Roberto sang Guantanamera, written by Jose Marti, a Cuban revolutionary leader fighting for independence from Spain in the late 1800s, in Spanish; and Bob did 'Sinatra.' Larry did his best singing, loud and a little off key, at the table.

A few months later, Larry decided to run for the King County Council. Larry's local district was heavily Democratic. It was a foregone conclusion that whoever won the Democratic primary would win the seat. Larry faced two formidable candidates in the Democratic primary--former television news reporter Barbara Stenson and former State Senator George Fleming. Fleming was also a leader in the African American community and it was widely speculated that Larry and Fleming would split the minority vote, allowing Stenson to win the seat. But it was Larry who took the primary to become a member of the King County Council.

And since that first election in 1991, Larry has run for re-election every four years and in each re-election campaign, he ran unopposed. As of the book's printing, Larry had announced plans to run again in 2015.

(Front) Larry, Roberto, translator, Alice Ito, and Bernie
(Back) Theresa Fujiwara, Cheryl Ellsworth, Bob, Don Williamson, 1992. Photo courtesy Santos collection

CHAPTER 30: Full Circle

In September of 1997, Bernie was diagnosed with colon cancer. The prognosis wasn't good, his doctors gave him six months to a year to live. Bernie was upbeat throughout his treatment and continued the work at Daybreak Star planning the development of the Peoples Lodge.

On November 1, 1997, Bernie's staff, family and close friends held a celebration of his life work at Union Station to thank him for the many memories each person shared with him through the many years. Worried that there was so little time to put a proper event together, the organizers wondered if renting the spacious Union Station was a little too ambitious, but the place was packed.

During the spring of 2000, the Four made it a point to be together for dinners on Sundays. Stories were retold better than the originals. Bernie stepped up his teasing of Roberto, who, in turn, would pick on Bob while Larry couldn't figure out if the other three were serious. Everybody shared "Bernie stories."

Claudia Kauffman told one such story, at that time, the Deputy Manager of the Daybreak Star Center.

She said that one morning, as Bernie drove to work at Daybreak Star Center, he heard a news flash on his car radio. He heard the announcer say that a "thousand Cherokees" were surrounding the Nation's Capital in Washington DC. The radio was not working well and there was a lot of static. Bernie was excited that the Native Americans were again on the warpath. He was going to purchase airline tickets immediately and fly back to support the Cherokees. He wanted to be part of the last great Indian War in the nation. Excitedly, he called his staff on his cell phone and asked them to turn on the television to a news channel. He was on his way and would be there in minutes.

Bernie and actor Will Sampson, best known for his role as Chief in *One Flew Over the Cuckoo's Nest* circa late 1970s. Photo courtesy UIATF

Bernie arrived at the Daybreak Star Center, jumped out of his car, and as he ran to the entrance, one of his staff members stopped him with this advice, "Relax, Bear, the newsman was not talking about Cherokees, he was talking about cherry trees." A thousand cherry trees surrounding the nation's Capital were in bloom.

Bernie shook his head and walked to his office somewhat confused and disappointed. He murmured, "Cherry trees? I could have sworn they were talking about Cherokees!"

Bernie fought the colon cancer for three years. He continued working on his dream project, the People's Lodge. He wanted to live long enough to see the Lodge become a reality. But the cancer finally caught up to Bernie and his health began to deteriorate. Everyone knew it was serious when Bernie stopped going to work.

On Sunday July 9, 2000, which coincidentally was Roberto's birthday, the Four with other family and friends celebrated with a BBQ for Bernie. It would be the last time the Four would be together. Bernie passed away on July 16, 2000.

At the memorial service, a thousand family and friends attended, among them were Senators Daniel Inouye and Patty Murray, Governors Gary Locke and Mike Lowry, King County Executive Ron Sims, Seattle Mayor Paul Schell, tribal chairs from almost every tribe in Washington, and hundreds of admirers.

Roberto, Larry, and Bob, along with Victor Johns, Bernie's best friend and John Daniels, then Chairman of the Muckleshoot Tribal Council, were among the pallbearers. As the casket was rolled into the hearse, a strong gust of wind blew a large canvas divider up into the air. All those around said, "There goes Bernie."

The remaining three continued to stay in touch, sharing the stage at fund-raising dinners, campaign receptions and family gatherings. They performed a musical number at an annual dinner for the Center for Career Alternatives. They each spoke at several early gatherings during the first Obama for President campaign.

Once a year, Jane Nishita, director of community affairs with U.S. West, hosted a dinner evening with Larry, Bob, and Roberto at a Mariners home game and a Sounders home game to hear for herself, the banter that went on between the remaining three.

It was during these times that Roberto and Bob challenged each other. Roberto would say to Bob, "I heard you were a boxer in the old days. Do you think you can beat me now?" Bob would reply, "I heard you were a street fighter in the old days. Street fighting and boxing are two different sports. In other words you wouldn't be able to put a glove on me." This challenge went on for years.

When Roberto injured his ankle in a pick-up basketball game and attended an event hobbling on a crutch, Bob ran up to him and yelled, "Now, Roberto, lets get it in on now!" Roberto responded, "Okay it's a deal, cuz I broke a bone in my foot not my chin."

In 2004, much to the surprise and amazement of all, Roberto was selected to become King Neptune for Seafair, Seattle's great summer festival. The honor of being King Neptune traditionally had gone to a city leader from the corporate or business sector.

There was Roberto, sitting on stage with Navy Captains, Admirals, Marine Corps Generals and other regional leaders. As the Navy's famous Blue Angels flew overhead, with his arm raised and pumping his fist in the air, Roberto yelled, "This show of power is a waste of the tax payer's money and the influence of the Industrial Military Complex on this people's celebration!" He was yelling this as two hundred thousand people were screaming for more of the Blue Angels.

In 2005, Bob received a call from the Executive Director of the Partners for Livable Communities, a national organization based in Washington D.C. Partners for Livable Communities is a non-profit organization working to improve the livability of communities by promoting quality of life, economic development and social equality. It has sponsored the Bridge Builders Award since 1997.

The Award is given to a man or a woman who nurtures hope, fosters partnership among segments of the community and possesses a vision of the future that transcends barriers of race, culture, language, geography and economic status. The National Coalition of Asian American and Pacific Islanders Community Development had submitted Bob's name for nomination for the Bridge Builders Award.

Honorees of the prestigious Bridge Builders award for 1997 to 2005 included: former president William J. Clinton; Emanuel Cleaver II, former mayor of Kansas City; Maynard H. Jackson, former mayor of Atlanta; Earvin "Magic" Johnson of the NBA; Congressman John Lewis, Georgia; Bette Midler, actress and founder of the New York Restoration Society; and Norm Mineta, former member of Congress and former Secretary of U.S Department of Transportation.

It was felt that the contribution and work of the Gang of Four merited national attention. Bob suggested that the Gang of Four, together in partnership with the MEDC, be given the Bridge Builders Award. The nomination read that the award was given "for their ability to bring disparate voices together into a chorus of possibility that works toward the goals of social well-being, economic opportunity and individual pride in oneself and one's neighbors."

Larry, Roberto, Bob, Kecia Reyes representing Bernie, and Dorry Elias-Garcia representing MEDC, were presented their awards at a black tie dinner where guests paid $1000 per plate. Although this type of expense for a dinner was new to the group, lobbyists and other philanthropic interests were used to attending these types of dinners. The Gang of Four and MEDC were guests so they were given a table to bring others to fill in.

The group from Seattle filled two tables with the Muckleshoot Tribe sponsoring the second table. As they were being called up by the emcee, former Seattle Mayor Charles Royer, to receive their awards, the two tables rose in unison and shouted with fists raised "the people united will never be defeated." A stunned Royer frowned then burst out laughing.

The last order of business on this trip to the nation's Capitol was a visit to the National Museum of the American Indian. Bernie was one of the founders and was very proud to be on the national board. This stunning museum, a part of the Smithsonian Institution, with the artifacts and written history of the American Indian movement, should be a destination for every American who visits Washington D.C. The exhibits on display come from every region of the country with most tribes represented. Visuals and written history with media presentations are part of the beautiful and graphic almost life-like images of the First People's struggles, victories, and realities.

In 2009, the YMCA of Greater Seattle selected the Gang of Four as the recipient of the A.K. Guy Award. During the ceremony, they were referred to as "Seattle's Fantastic Four." The program listed them as "Fighting for Truth and Justice, The Seattle Way."

The testimonial noted that "the four are among the most influential and charismatic leaders in our community. Their activism for social justice and civil rights has changed the face of leadership in the Puget Sound region. Their vision for fully integrating minorities into the area's social, economic and political life has inspired generations as well as helped create Seattle's reputation as a place where every individual can make a difference."

In 2010, after Roberto's annual medical check up, his doctor advised him that surgery was required immediately, and checked him into the hospital the next day. He had cancer. As all fighters do, Roberto fought to overcome the cancer that was riddling his body. Although in constant treatment, Roberto led his usual grueling pace as Executive Director of El Centro but, as the saying goes, all good things must end and Roberto stepped down after handing over the ship to Estela Ortega.

As time was running out and Roberto began to slow down, a wonderful thing happened. Anne Levinson, a part owner of the Seattle Storm professional women's basketball team, invited Roberto to a Storm playoff game at Key Arena, and introduced Roberto to the sold-out crowd at half time. She then brought Roberto to meet each team member in the locker room after the game, which the Storm won.

A stunning photo of Roberto by Tacoma-based photographer Gilbert W. Arias

On September 22, 2010, after years of treatment, Roberto passed away. His memorial service and wake were attended by thousands of supporters and family members. The Seattle Mayor's Office, where he and others had been arrested 37 years previously, ordered flags flown at half-mast the day he died.

EPILOGUE

By Norm Rice

Now there are two. As of this printing, Larry is still serving on the Martin Luther King Jr. County Council as the longest serving councilmember. He also co-chairs the annual Martin Luther King Jr. celebration march held at Garfield High School, a responsibility he has taken in each of the last twenty years. His co-chairs are student leaders of Garfield. Even while being a big player in local government, he has never compromised his outspoken position on human rights. He has never turned down an opportunity to speak at public events or in classrooms for students from all grades, including colleges and universities, about his life experiences.

Larry, along with King County Executive Ron Sims and former King County Councilmember Bruce Laing, were responsible for the renaming of King County after the Rev. Martin Luther King Jr., the only county in the country named after the civil rights leader.

Bob, although retired, still gives tours of the International District and lectures about his experiences in the preservation and development of the International District, and his years serving in government as an aide to Congressman Mike Lowry, and as Regional Administrator for the Department of Housing and Urban Development. In December of 2012, he took his first trip to the Philippines to accept the prestigious Overseas Filipino 'Banaag Award' from Philippine President Benigno Aquino.

Each member of the Gang of Four will be remembered for their unselfish dedication and commitment to their respective communities. These communities were made stronger because of their willingness to join forces with other communities of color and progressive movements that started in the sixties and continues to this day.

Nowhere else in the country has there been a foursome quite like the Gang of Four who started at the height of the civil rights movement and brought together the activists from their respective communities.

As the Gang of Four, "Four Amigos," or "Fantastic Four," they blazed trails, fought the fight, won the respect of every sector of the community and they did it with charm, grace, energy, humor, dignity and love.

"The People, United, Will Never Be Defeated -- El Pueblo Unido Jamás Será Vencido!"

The Gang Of Four with Cheryl Ellsworth on their way to Japan.
Photo by Theresa Fujiwara

ACKNOWLEDGEMENTS

I would like to thank my wife, Sharon Tomiko, for her input, support and understanding through this long journey — patiently helping me through my one-finger attempts to type on my tablet while writing this book. She was also very close to each member of the Gang of Four.

I can't give enough credit to my co-author, Gary Iwamoto, who did much of the research and writing. It was several years ago when Gary, along with Elaine Ikoma Ko, met with Roberto, Larry, and myself after Bernie passed away, to begin documenting the legacy of the Gang of Four. Several meetings were held, a video session was shot, and then the story hung in limbo until Roberto passed.

It was then that Larry and I realized the sense of urgency that this story needed to be written without any further delays.

This book would still be in our minds if it were not for Elaine who answered my call for assistance in coordinating this entire project. "It takes a village" and I am eternally grateful to "our village" which included our sponsors John Daniels of the Muckleshoot IndianTribe and Joseph Martin, Director of the Muckleshoot Education Department; Bruce Rutledge, our publisher, working with Chelsey Slattum; John Santos of Zeus Design for our book design; and Sean Muliro for the web design.

Much credit goes to the other remaining member of the Gang of Four, Larry Gossett, who shared long-lasting memories of his past and to his long-time Chief of Staff Cindy Domingo for her part in gently encouraging timely responses from Larry despite his busy schedule. Extra blessings to Larry's wife, Rhonda Gossett, for being there for Larry and us.

A very hearty thanks to Estella Ortega who now leads El Centro de la Raza and shares a large part of this history. I would also like to commend her for her saintly devotion to Roberto, who I imagine would have been very difficult to keep up with, and thanks to Miguel Maestas for sharing photos and stories from the El Centro archives.

Many thanks to Bernie's sister, Laura Whitebear, for her input and to Bernie's brother, Lawney Reyes who allowed us to use passages from his book, "Bernie Whitebear: An Urban Indian's Quest For Justice," published in 2006, and for the photos they provided for this book.

Doug Chin shared his memories of us in the book's Foreword and several years earlier, Melissa Lin provided the initial framework for our story. Theresa Fujiwara and Alice Ito brought the four of us to Japan and should be given a special award for keeping us all on track throughout Japan. A special salute to Professor Bruce Johansen for providing a short history of our sponsor, the Muckleshoot Indian Tribe.

I want to acknowledge Pio DeCano, Jr. who sent me the quote below about his late father who, in my recollection as a young boy learned through my Uncle Joe Adriatico, that Pio DeCano, Sr. fought for and won his civil rights case in the early 1940's. He was my first hero.

"Pio DeCano, Sr. defied the prohibitive warning found on many west coast rental facilities "Positively No Filipinos Allowed," and challenged the law that denied ownership of land by Filipino-Americans in Washington State, winning his case in the State's Supreme Court in 1941. The decision changed the course of Filipino-American community development, locally, nationally and internationally forever."

A special acknowledgment goes to Eddie Rye, Jr. for sharing his memories of places and events for this book. He was with Tyree Scott and each member of the Gang of Four from the very beginning, participating in the meetings, rallies, demonstrations (many which he led) and we especially enjoyed his company when sitting in our jail cells before our court appearances. To this day, he continues to keep public officials at their word.

Thanks to Henry Cisneros, former Secretary of the U.S. Department of Housing and Urban Development and my former boss, for writing words of encouragement in support of this book and his faith in me when we opened the Federal Building in Seattle as a shelter for homeless women.

A hearty thank you to Mike Lowry, former Washington State Governor and former member of Congress, who allowed me to replace him on the three-member delegation that successfully negotiated the release of eight Salvadorian human rights officials from their prisons in El Salvador.

Michael Woo contributed words of encouragement and shared his experiences while working with Tyree Scott at the United Construction Workers Association and appreciation goes to Diane Narasaki for her decades of support for us.

And finally, thank you to Scott Gutiérrez of U.S. Senator Maria Cantwell's office and Senator Cantwell for their support of this book.

-Bob Santos

ABOUT THE BOOK SPONSOR

The Muckleshoot Indian Tribe, with its reservation located in Auburn, Washington, is a federally recognized Indian tribe whose membership is composed of descendants of the Duwamish and Upper Puyallup people who inhabited Central Puget Sound for thousands of years before non-Indian settlement.

The Tribe's name is derived from the native name for the prairie on which the Muckleshoot Reservation was established. Following the Reservation's establishment in 1857, the Tribe and its members came to be known as Muckleshoot, rather than by the historic tribal names of their Duwamish and Upper Puyallup ancestors. Today, the United States recognizes the Muckleshoot Tribe as a tribal successor to the Duwamish and Upper Puyallup bands from which the Tribe's membership descends.

The Muckleshoot Tribe takes great pride in their important role in Washington state. The Tribe has grown to become one of the largest employers in southeast King County and the economic impact of various business ventures is significant.

Through their Charity Fund and Community Impact contributions, the Tribe provides almost $3 million annually to local governments, schools, churches and non-profit organizations. The Tribe's role as co-manager of the natural resources in this area benefits the entire region.

On behalf of the Tribal Council and all Muckleshoot people, we are pleased to support this important book "Gang of Four." We hope that many readers will come to understand and learn about the contributions of these four leaders and the many they inspired, and who made great strides in racial and social justice for all.

The Tribe welcomes guests to visit our casino or Bingo Hall, attend a concert at the White River Amphitheatre, enjoy a stay at the Salish Lodge and Spa, or just visit the reservation. The Tribe appreciates your friendship and support.

IN THEIR HONOR

Gang of Four

- Bridge Builders 2005, from Partners for Livable Communities, Washington DC
- A.K. Guy Award 2009, from Seattle YMCA
- Leadership Award 2014, from Compassionate Seattle

Bob Santos

In 2004, Santos Place opened, named after Bob Santos. Santos Place, currently operated by the Low Income House Institute, offers 42 transitional housing units for single homeless men and women including veterans with three ADA-accessible units. Santos Place is located in the Sand Point neighborhood in Seattle.

Larry Gossett

In 2011, Gossett Place opened, named after Larry Gossett. Gossett Place, currently operated by the Low Income Housing Institute, offers 62 units of housing for homeless veterans and young single men and women. Gossett Place is located in the University District in Seattle.

Bernie Whitebear

In 2011, the City of Seattle renamed Lawton Wood Boulevard "Bernie Whitebear Way" on the road that leads to the Daybreak Star Center at Discovery Park in Seattle.

Roberto Maestas

In 2011, the Seattle City Council unanimously passed the naming of South Lander Street between 16th Avenue South and 17th Avenue South, the street than runs adjacent to El Centro de la Raza, to "South Roberto Maestas Festival Street" in Seattle.

On March 6, 2015, El Centro held a gound breaking ceremony for *Plaza Roberto Maestas Beloved Community*, a multi-use housing, education, social service and retail develpment.

Santos Place

Gossett Place

Bernie Whitebear Way

Artist rendering of the future Plaza Roberto Maestas
Beloved Community

Artist rendering of the future Plaza Roberto Maestas
Beloved Community

INDEX